In *Encountering Angels*, Jeran
ing in kingdom power; almost daring you to ......
power broker of the Holy Spirit and learn to partner with angels
that are constantly in your midst, whether you see them or not.
This book is a prophetic word to this generation.

JULIA LOREN, Author of *Shifting Shadows of Supernatural Power*,
The Future of Us, and *Claim Your Anointing*

Jerame Nelson is amazing! I am always excited when he puts out a
new book because I know that the high-watermark of the kingdom
will be challenged. He operates in such incredible supernatural
faith that all of his books stir up and challenge you to reach for
more. Finally, his book on angels is here—prepare to be stretched!

PROFESSOR JONATHAN WELTON, TH.D., Best-Selling Author and
Founder of The Welton Academy

Angels are real and they *are* among us—the Bible says so. Jerame
Nelson shares personal encounters and gives scriptural teaching
on the angels that labor among us. You might be surprised to find
that there have been angels in your midst that you were not aware
of. I recommend this eye-opening book to anyone who is hungry
to understand more about the angels of heaven. It's a great read.

PATRICIA KING, XPmedia.com

We are not alone! God's heavenly army is ready to assist you in
your life and ministry today. Join Jerame Nelson in faith and believe that "greater are they who are with us than they who are in
the world."

JAMES W GOLL, Encounters Network

JERAME NELSON

ENCOUNTERING
ANGELS

REAL-LIFE EXPERIENCES
OF HEAVENLY INTERVENTION

Authentic

•

Published by Authentic Publishers
188 Front Street, Suite 116-44
Franklin, TN 37064

Authentic Publishers is a division of Authentic Media, Inc.

Library of Congress Cataloging-in-Publication Data
Nelson, Jerame
    Encountering Angels : Real-life experiences of heavenly intervention / Jerame Nelson
p. cm.

ISBN 978-1-78078-135-8
    978-1-78078-375-8 (eBook)

Printed in the United States of America
22 21 20 19 18 17 16 15   10 9 8 7 6 5 4 3 2 1

I would like to dedicate this book
to my amazing wife Miranda.

*Thank you for being my wife, best friend,
faithful supporter, and co-laborer in the ministry.
Thank you for walking with me on this
amazing adventure of preaching the supernatural
gospel of Jesus Christ to the nations of this world.
You have encouraged, trusted and believed in
me to go deeper in my pursuit of God.
You truly are a Proverb 31 woman
and I love you so much.*

CONTENTS

FOREWORD

We see the presence of angels showing up in dreams, visitations and encounters. The history of the entire Gospel was shaped through angelic activity. Today it may not be as common to hear about angelic visitations and encounters, but they exist and are happening right in our midst! In fact, there are more accounts of supernatural activity in the body of Christ today then in the centuries proceeding. Why now? Why is there a heightened awareness of angelic beings? The answer is because God is preparing us for the great harvest, and we cannot do it alone!

I have never had the amazing experience of seeing angels with my physical sight, but I have no doubt encountered their presence. In fact, much of my existence today is due not just to the guidance of the Holy Spirit, but also to the help of angels. It was at the University of Maryland where I believe I encountered an intervention that possibly saved my life. I was walking with some college friends on campus when out of nowhere a speeding motorcycle hit me in my back, catapulting me through the air. As I skidded to a violent stop on the concrete, my college buddies thought I was dead.

I should have been dead, or seriously injured. Instead, I gingerly stood up without a scratch on me; not even my clothes were tarnished from being run over. I believe angels were there to protect me, maybe even my guardian angel. Although I did not see any angels, I know their presence was there to protect me.

I've also had what I believe was a Macedonian call to come to California back in the '80s. A large African American man appeared to me in a dream and told me to "come to California, for there will be a great harvest." It was the prompting from what I believe was the angel of Los Angeles that brought me here from the East Coast. Through the confirmation of my leadership, I obeyed and have been living here in Southern California since 1984.

Then there was my 2007 dream of angels. In it, I saw many harvest angels coming out of the water carrying harvest nets. And I heard in my spirit the scripture, "Be(ing) diligent to preserve the unity of the Spirit in the bond of peace" (Ephesians 4:3, NASB). The Lord gave me these two dreams to encourage my spirit, but also to instruct me and guide me in my ministry walk. The angels that appeared in my dreams were messenger angels.

Jerame's book is a great guide to the angelic realm because it explains the different kinds of angels and their purposes. You will be encouraged and provoked by the passion and obedience of this young revivalist as he illustrates his personal stories. The testimonies you read will ignite a hunger for the supernatural that you may not have yet seen in your life.

If you are looking for greater visitation in you personal life, family, and city, this book will give you the tools to activate your supernatural senses. I am confident that as you journey through each chapter, you will begin to see more doors open in creative and supernatural realms. It will help build faith to experience your own encounters. You will also gain biblical understanding about where angels originated from and their purposes here on earth.

Buckle your seat belts for the ride and expect God to do amazing things in your life today. And get ready to position yourself for angelic visitations!

Dr. Ché Ahn, Senior Pastor, HRock Church, Pasadena, CA
President, Harvest International Ministry
International Chancellor, Wagner Leadership Institute

1

ANGELS AMONG US

One afternoon, while on our way to a shopping district in downtown Vancouver, from the small city of Abbotsford, British Columbia, my wife and I noticed an unusual man walking down the street—or rather, crutching down the street.

As he reached his crutches forward, he stepped out with one good leg, but dragged the other along the asphalt. He could hardly crutch across the road. It is natural for us to notice those in need of healing and we tuned into the opportunity to see another miracle happen to a total stranger. Our shopping excursion could wait.

We decided to stop and pray for him to get healed, so I pulled our car into a parking space across from where the man was crossing the street. We got out of the car and stood waiting, expectantly. It took quite some time for him to cross the road.

When he finally reached the curb and walked onto the sidewalk, we approached and told him we were Christians, and that we believe that Jesus heals. We then asked if we could pray for him to be healed.

He ended up saying *yes* and told us the problem was with his hip. So we laid hands on the man and started praying for God to heal him.

After we were done we asked the man to do something he could not do before, and check to see if he was healed. In response, the man pulled up his shirt and showed us his hip. Much to my surprise, he had no hip at all. There was just a big, deformed-looking hole where his hip was supposed to be. When I saw this, all of my faith immediately fled out down the sidewalk drains. It's easy to pray for someone when you are not looking at the natural cause of the disability—when you look at what is unseen rather than what is seen. But it's much harder when you stare at the problem raw and real, up close and personal.

> I believe that honoring the anointing of those who came before us will enable us to receive an impartation of their anointing.

The man shifted the conversation away from his disability and told us a little about his life. "I am so blessed that you stopped to pray for me! I am a Christian too, and my great grandfather was the man of God who started the Pentecostal church in Canada," he said.

When I heard this, I thought, *We should be getting this man to lay hands on us, not us laying hands on him.* I believe that honoring the anointing of those who came before us will enable us to receive an impartation of their anointing—even if it comes through the prayers of one who is descended from that anointed man or woman of God.

As if he knew my thoughts, this man said to both my wife and me, "Can I pray for you guys?" Of course we said yes and stepped closer to him. He placed one hand on each of us and prayed that we would receive an anointing for miracles, signs and wonders, and then went on to prophesy things that only wife, God, and I could know! It was powerful. At the end, he gave us a huge hug and said he needed to go.

So we got into our car and turned around to look back on the road, but much to our surprise the man had vanished into thin air! It had only been 30 seconds tops since we hugged the man and turned around. Yet, this slow-moving man had just simply vanished. I jumped out of the car and looked for him down every street in the intersection, but could not find him. No cars had passed by, and there were no doors into which he could have entered and disappeared.

As I was looking, the Holy Spirit spoke to me saying, You won't find him. He was an angel. I sent him to test your hearts and activate in you more of the fire of God for the miraculous.

Then the Lord told me to tell the people of God to get ready, because you never know when He might be testing our hearts and entertaining angels who walk among us in many forms. We have to always be living with our spiritual antennas up; God is always looking to see if we really live what we say we believe. When this encounter took place I had been crying out for more of God's power and authority to see miracles in the streets and our ministry. As a result, I believe God sent the "man" to test our hearts. When we stopped to pray for him, I got exactly what I had asked for: a blessing that increased the anointing.

I believe God tests our hearts to see just how obedient we are to His voice. God is looking for friends to whom He can entrust the precious things of His kingdom. Sometimes God will ask you to stop for the one in front of you, even when it is inconvenient. The result of obedience however, will release the kingdom of God in our midst as God rewards those who diligently seek Him and follow His leading.

The day following that encounter with the angel, I prayed about the man and what God had said to me. The encounter awakened a desire in me to search out the role of angels in our lives. While in prayer, the Holy Spirit immediately reminded me of a key principle contained in Hebrews 13:1-2, which reads, "Let brotherly love continue. Do not forget to entertain strangers, for by so doing some have unwittingly entertained angels."

Then the Lord drew to mind a story in the Old Testament about how two angels appeared to Lot outside his home in Sodom and Gomorrah. They were visible to everyone in the city; apparently, these angels took the appearance of men.

The men of that city wanted to launch a lascivious attack on the angels, so Lot brought them into his house, rescuing them from the gang outside (see Genesis 19: 1-5). This angry gang of men didn't recognize that these two visitors were angels, and wanted to have their way with them. Lot intervened, however, and was ultimately rewarded for his efforts.

While researching angels in Scripture, I again heard the voice of God impress upon me to study the presence and role of all of the angels in the Bible. He expressed that if His people began to understand what the Word of God says about angels and their importance in the kingdom, they would experience greater breakthrough in their personal lives, cities, regions, and nations.

After I studied the role of angels, I immediately saw breakthrough in my own life and ministry. Soon after my study of angels in the Scriptures, I traveled to Korea to speak and minister, and experienced an angelic visitation. As I was praying about what to speak on in an upcoming meeting, an angel dressed in traditional Korean clothes appeared to me. The angel revealed that one of the major strongholds of Korea was religious thinking. The angel showed me that many Koreans had not yet renewed their minds to the things of the spirit of God. I told the pastor of the Church I

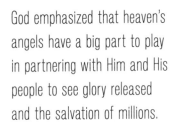

God emphasized that heaven's angels have a big part to play in partnering with Him and His people to see glory released and the salvation of millions.

was speaking at about the vision, and she told me that the revelation I received was correct. She emphasized that the biggest stronghold holding Koreans back from knowing God's love and presence was a religious mindset. That weekend, I focused my messages on the biblical process of renewing one's mind, opening to the love of God, and entering into the reality of the Holy Spirit.

As I ministered, many people were set free from religious mindsets and encountered the presence and power of the Holy Spirit for the first time. As a result of my own angelic visitation, I was able to accurately minister a word in season to the people of the church; it was an enormous blessing to see hundreds of people open up to godly dreams, visions, and His holy power.

The Lord also told me that His glory was about to invade the earth, and that millions of souls were going to come to salvation in the near future. God emphasized that heaven's angels have a big part to play in partnering with Him and His people to see glory released and the salvation of millions.

My friends, the goal of this book is to demystify the realm of the angelic and bring you into a greater understanding of their role and function in God's plan of salvation. My prayer is that you will be equipped to do the work of the ministry by partnering with God and His amazing variety of angels, in order to see an awesome end-time harvest of souls.

THE WORD OF THE LORD FOR YOU:

+ *Get ready because you never know when I, the Lord your God might be testing your heart and you might be entertaining angels who walk among you in many forms.*

+ *If you begin to understand what my Word says about angels and their importance in the kingdom, you will experience greater breakthrough in your personal life, as well as in your city, region, and nation.*

+ *My glory is about to invade earth and millions of souls are going to come to salvation in the near future. The angels of heaven have a big part to play in partnering with me and you to see this glory released and the salvation of millions come to pass.*

2

ANGELS TAKE HUMAN FORM

The meeting with the angel on crutches was not my first encounter with the angelic realm. My previous encounters had been confined to angels appearing to me in visions or dreams. Since then, I've seen angels and heavenly beings appear in many forms. However, it was that angel on crutches who changed my perspective on just how real and tangible the kingdom of God could become. This was my first encounter with an angel who appeared as a man in the natural world.

Let me tell you about another encounter where another angel appeared to a pastor and told the pastor about me—long before I ever met the pastor.

It happened around two years before interacting with the angel on crutches.

At the time I was home in Grand Junction, Colorado visiting my family for the summer before heading off to Canada on a fall ministry internship. At the time, I would take any invitation that would come my way. I was just getting launched into ministry and received an invitation to speak at a small home group in Montrose, Colorado. So I gladly accepted the invite and drove out to Montrose to meet with the leader of the home group. We had lunch and some hangout time to get to know each other before the evening meeting started.

During lunch, I was shocked as the pastor began to tell me about a friend of his who claimed to have met me on a plane the previous week. He described how I told the man my testimony about giving up baseball to preach, and how I had been wearing a red Boston Red Sox hat and a red sweatshirt on the plane. This was actually my favorite hat and the description of a sweatshirt I often wore at that time.

It made me realize that although, to my knowledge, I had not yet seen or talked with an angel, an angel certainly knew me.

There was only one problem with this guy's story: I had not been on an airplane for more than two months.

Who was the mystery man who talked with this pastor's friend? And why? It quickly became apparent that the man's friend knew way too much about me for this to be a coincidence or case of mistaken identity. I knew that something supernatural had taken place; and it blew my mind when I realized that angels were at work on my behalf. It made me realize that although, to my knowledge, I had not yet seen or talked with an angel, an angel certainly knew me. I prayed about it and searched the Bible for an explanation.

I found the story in Luke 24 when Jesus appeared to the two disciples on the road to Emmaus, and came to them in a form they did not recognize. I thought, *That's what must have happened. Jesus came in another form and appeared to the pastor's friend in my appearance.* Having satisfied myself with that explanation, I left it at that.

But then I realized that the passage in Luke 24 was about *Jesus* appearing. I realized that it probably wasn't Jesus who appeared to the man and spoke about me. Therefore, it must have been an angel! All of a sudden it all made sense.

I could not help but wonder if God supernaturally was working behind the scene to shift me to the place where I needed to be in ministry. God is excellent at opening doors and establishing us into our callings. Perhaps one of the reasons God sent the angel to this pastor-friend was to prompt him to invite me to speak. God is the best networker.

At the beginning of my ministry, I wasn't receiving hundreds of invitations through my website to speak in churches and at conferences. In fact, I didn't have a website. I just prayed for God to open the door for any opportunity for me to minister. We can be confident in the fact that even if man does not know who we are, our Father does and He will create opportunities. God opens up the doors for ministry in creative ways that are not our ways.

Doors can open when He sends an angel, or enables your gifts to shine into the hearts of others, which makes room for your ministry. Some of us need to stop striving to make things happen. I was content with speaking or not speaking, leaving the promotion up to God. My focus was to spend as much time as I could with Jesus, focusing on His presence and reading the Word. As you fix your eyes on Jesus, He will open doors that no man can open—and He can do it supernaturally.

In the ten years since the airplane event, angels have facilitated miracles in many meetings, and helped release the word that I was to speak. Through this process of experiencing angelic visitations in a corporate setting, God has also taught me how to flow with angels when they do appear. I've had such angelic encounters during ministry times on platforms, and in the streets when praying for people. As well, I have witnessed how such encounters can cause shifts in the spiritual atmosphere over a city, or help herald impending events.

But before all these encounters began, I first needed to search out the role of angels in Scripture and become comfortable with their presence among us. Only through God's Word could I learn to partner with them for the sake of my life and for the sake of those to whom I ministered. For the Word says, "Are not all angels ministering spirits sent to serve those who will inherit salvation?" (Hebrews 1:14, NIV)

As I began to study all the angelic visitations found in the Bible, the Lord spoke to me about how He was about to release more encounters with the angelic realm to the body of Christ than ever before. It is His will that heaven invades earth; an "army of angels" is currently being sent to help the saints bring the fullness of His salvation to pass.

When the Holy Spirit spoke about this to me, I was reminded of how Jesus taught his disciples to pray. In Matthew 6:9-10, Jesus said to his disciples, "In this manner, therefore, pray: 'Our Father in heaven, hallowed be Your name. Your kingdom come. Your will be done on earth as it is in heaven.'"

What did Jesus mean when He said *your will be done on earth as it is in heaven*? I believe that He literally meant what He said: that the will of heaven would come to earth—and that includes the angelic realm as well.

Many people are preaching and teaching about heaven invading earth. Most of that teaching is centered on the principles of salvation, healing, deliverance, peace and joy for the individual. Not much of it focuses on the visitation side of heaven invading earth. However, the Bible is full of stories of heaven invading earth in the form of face-to-face encounters with God, as well as with the angelic realm. Do you realize how vital the role angels played throughout the Bible and especially in the New Testament church?

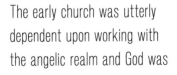

The early church was utterly dependent upon working with the angelic realm and God was constantly sending angels to release His word to people in both Old and New Testaments.

The early church was utterly dependent upon working with the angelic realm and God was constantly sending angels to release His word to people in both Old and New Testaments. Why would it not be equally important to partner with angels—and receive them—in our time and day? As I searched out angels in the word of God, and especially the book of Acts, I began to realize that angelic encounters were quite a normal thing in the culture of the early church. They were used to having encounters with angels! They needed them to save their lives, and to help them save others.

In Acts chapter 12, for example, Peter was arrested and thrown into prison for preaching the gospel. He had been sentenced to death and thrown into jail, but because it was the Sabbath, the executioners had to wait until the next day to kill Peter. So the head of the prison tightened up the security and added some extra guards to watch over Peter for the night.

Meanwhile the followers of Jesus were at Mary's house praying for God to save Peter from prison. They lifted up their voices in prayer and cried out to God. Unbeknownst to them, God answered immediately by sending an angel to Peter in prison. The angel woke up Peter and supernaturally led him out of the high security prison to safety. Peter saw the angels and thought he was dreaming. But once he stepped foot out of the prison, he knew that he was free; this was no dream. Then he fled to the house of Mary, where he knew his friends had assembled in prayer.

He knocked on the door and a servant girl named Rhoda answered, heard Peter's voice, and became very excited. She saw him, then slammed the door in his face and ran in to tell the group that God had answered their prayers and released Peter from prison. As she told the group that Peter was outside the door waiting, a puzzling thing happened. Instead of having faith that God really answered their prayers, they said, "'You are beside yourself!' Yet she kept insisting that it was so. So they said, 'It is his angel'" (Acts 12:15).

What? Hold up a minute. So they had more faith that Peter's angel was at the door than in the possibility that God had answered their prayers and released Peter from prison? Wow—what a shocker!

After thinking about this for a while, I realized that the appearance of angels must have been a fairly common supernatural event for them. It also seems likely from the story in Acts 12 that angels could appear as everyday, ordinary people.

It seems apparent from the biblical record that there were more supernatural events in the early years after Christ's death and resurrection than what we experience in today's expression of Christianity. What an amazing God we serve that He would send an angel on a guardian assignment to release Peter from a life-or-death situation. Today's church must begin to understand the angelic realm of God, particularly as violence toward Christians rises around the globe. I can now clearly see how the angelic realm is sent from heaven to administrate the goodness and glory of God in the earth.

After reading this account of Peter I realized there is a good chance that we have personal angels who look like us. Why else would those in Mary's house say to Rhoda, "It is his angel" (Acts 12:15)?

There are angels who save us from being harmed; angels who look like us; and angels who watch over us. They know everything about us, and are able to intervene in our lives by taking human form—whether we recognize them as angels or as mere humans. We think on an encounter and wonder if it was an angel, then dismiss it as, "Nah, it was just a person." Pay attention to your encounters

> Today's church must begin to understand the angelic realm of God, particularly as violence toward Christians rises around the globe.

with others. Pay attention to those who have encountered someone you may think was a mere man or woman, but was likely an angel in human form.

I love the following account of an angelic encounter that Billy Graham's father-in-law had while living as a missionary in China. This story is taken from Billy Graham's exceptional book *Angels*:

My wife, Ruth, tells of a strange incident in a Christian book room in Shanghai, China. She learned of it through her father, the late Dr. L. Nelson Bell who served in the hospital in Tsing-kiangpu, Jiangsu province. It was at this store that Dr. Bell bought his gospel portions and tracts to distribute among his patients. The incident occurred in 1942, after the Japanese had won control of certain areas of China.

One morning around nine o'clock, a Japanese truck stopped outside the bookroom. It was carrying five marines and was half-filled with books. The Christian Chinese shop assistant, who was alone at the time, realized with dismay that they had come to seize the stock. By nature timid, he felt this was more than he could endure. Jumping from the truck, the marines made for the shop door, but before they could enter, a neatly dressed Chinese gentleman entered the shop ahead of them.

Though the shop assistant knew practically all the Chinese customers who traded there, this man was a

26

complete stranger. For some unknown reason, the soldiers seemed unable to follow him, and loitered about, looking in at the four large windows, but not entering. For two hours they stood around, until after eleven, but never set foot inside the door.

The stranger asked what the men wanted, and the Chinese shop assistant explained that the Japanese were seizing stock from many of the bookshops in the city, and now this store's turn had come. The two prayed together, the stranger encouraging him, and so the two hours passed. At last the soldiers climbed into their truck and drove away.

The stranger also left, without making a single purchase or even inquiring about any items in the shop. Later that day the shop owner, Mr. Christopher Willis (whose Chinese name was Lee), returned. The shop assistant said to him, "Mr. Lee, do you believe in angels?"

"I do," said Mr. Willis. "So do I, Mr. Lee." Could the stranger have been one of God's protecting angels? Dr. Bell always thought so.[1]

I love this story. Here you can see an angel of protection that manifested itself in human form as it appeared like a customer of this bookshop. The end result was that the marines could not persecute or take the materials of God from this bookshop. We will be looking more at guardian (or protection) angels in the next chapter.

THE WORD OF THE LORD FOR YOU:

When you pray, pray like this: "Our Father in heaven, hallowed be Your name. Your kingdom come. Your will be done on earth as it is in heaven." And as you pray, let heaven invade earth. And I will release angels to open doors that confine you—in the natural and spiritual. I declare to you that no prison wall, no injustice will stand against my plans and purposes for you. I have sent my angels to watch over you, to guard you in all of your ways. I am sending angels ahead of you to open doors of opportunity that will enable you to walk into your anointing and release it in places that I have ordained for you. In Jesus' name, Amen.

3

VARIOUS KINDS
OF ANGELS

Have you ever seen an angel, or wondered whether you have? It could be you simply aren't aware that there are various kinds of angels or that God sends them to us on assignment. As you become aware of them, you will likely pay more attention and begin to see them on a regular basis. How do I know this? An expectation based on Scripture increases faith, and God responds to faith. God also responds to encourage our faith so we can increase in faith!

Hebrews 11 speaks about many men and women who received angelic visitations. This "faith hall of fame" chapter describes many biblical heroes whom God spoke to through angels, enabling each person to persevere through trials and hardships with a supernatural gift of faith. These angelic visitations served to increase the person's faith because God knew they were enduring tough circumstances and that such encounters would strengthen their faith.

Those who lived in the days of Old Testament and New Testament culture believed in the existence of angels—but like us, probably thought angelic visitations were reserved for "special people." Guess what? Those in the Bible who thought they were ordinary discovered that they were special. They were chosen to receive a visitation.

> Need more faith? Read the Word. And ask God to increase your faith.

The good news is that the Holy Spirit was poured out at Pentecost (see Acts 2) and is still being released today. That initial outpouring revealed the Spirit coming on *all* people—not just a chosen few (see Acts 2:4). The way is open for all of us to be "special" enough to receive angelic visitations through dreams, visions, and other forms. What does it take to enter into the realm of the Holy Spirit, the realm of God's kingdom here on earth?

Faith releases the presence and power of God. Faith comes from hearing—and reading—the Word of God (Romans 10:17). Need more faith? Read the Word. And ask God to increase your faith.

James 2:5 says this about God's promise to increase your faith: "Listen, my dear brothers and sisters: Has not God chosen those who are poor in the eyes of the world to be rich in faith and inherit the kingdom He promised those who love Him?" (NIV). Inheriting the kingdom means partaking freely of the supernatural realm where angels and spiritual creatures in heavenly places interact with us on earth as it is in heaven. As you study the role of angels in the Bible, you will begin to enter into the kingdom convergence of heaven invading your life. So, what are you expecting to see and experience?

MINISTERING SPIRITS

God's angels are ministering spirits sent to assist (or minister to) those who are to inherit salvation. This means that God is not limited by just human ministers, but has his own ministers that work under His command to accomplish what He desires in the earth and in the lives of His people.

The Bible mentions many types of angels and knowing some of the roles they play will help you understand how an angel might appear in your life. Some stories in Scripture give amazing details of what angels look like, and reveal their functions or assignments. As I studied I found there are watcher angels, healing angels, angels of joy, guardian angels, warring angels, messenger angels, living creatures, seraphim angels, cherubim angels, and many more. Lets look at a few of them.

MESSENGER ANGELS

The word for *angel* in the Greek is *ággelos,* which translates as *messenger.* God sent angels to many people in the Bible for all kinds of different reasons. Gabriel, one of the most important messenger angels, often shows up to make an announcement that has earth-shaking consequences. He was sent from heaven to Daniel (see Daniel 9) as well as to Zacharias, the father of John the Baptist (see Luke 1). He was even sent to announce the conception of Christ to Mary (Luke 1:26).

Sometimes, God will give us warning visitations to keep us out of trouble or to protect us from the plans of the devil. Matthew 2:12 tells us that Joseph, the father of Jesus, was divinely warned through an angelic encounter in a dream. He was told not to return to the land of Herod, but that he and Mary were to take Jesus to another country. The result was that Jesus' life was spared.

What would have happened if Joseph had not listened to the angel's warning? Jesus would have been killed by Herod's men, along with all male babies of Bethlehem up to two years of age.

Honoring a visitation in a dream or a vision is most important. It pays to listen to the Lord when He speaks. You never know what blessing is behind the door of obedience, or the consequences of ignoring a visitation or message.

God has sent angels to me in the form of warning dreams or visions many times. In one such dream, I saw a minister friend get into a very serious car accident. As I woke up from the dream I knew I was called to pray that God would release His angels to protect this man. So I went to one of my spiritual mentors and asked him to pray with me. We bound the plans of the enemy and prayed for God's angels of protection to be released.

A few hours later, we received a phone call from this man's ministry office saying that my friend had been in an accident and broken his leg. I was so glad we were obedient to pray for him. Who knows how much worse it could have been if we had not prayed? I believe that God will visit us sometimes via angelic visitation in our dreams so that we can partner with Him in prayer and cancel the plans of the enemy.

Sometimes as a minister, it's not just about receiving a warning from God; it's about receiving a message from God for the people to whom you are ministering. This happened to me one evening when

I was praying in my home in San Diego. That night I was asking God for more of the Holy Spirit and for an increase in visitations and ability to hear His voice.

Out of nowhere, I fell into a trance and had a vision of an angel holding a massive pearl that seemed to be the size of a softball. As I looked at this beautiful pearl, I saw that it was encased in what looked like a massive flame of fire. The pearl seemed to be burning with fire all around it. As I took note of this in the encounter, something special happened. The angel extended his hands toward me and placed this stunning pearl into the palms of my hands. I could feel the fire of God all around me as I held the pearl.

> The key to receiving more of the power and visitation of God was to sell out to the presence of God's fire.

When I came out of the encounter I was right back in my living room again. Afterward, the Holy Spirit began to speak to me about the significance of the vision. He said, "Tell the people of God that if they want to obtain the precious things of My Kingdom, they must embrace the fire of God." When the Holy Spirit spoke this to me, I knew He was giving me the answer to my prayers that night. I knew He wanted me to share this message wherever I would be ministering in that season. I also realized that the key to receiving more of the power and visitation of God was to sell out to the presence of God's fire.

I also learned through this encounter that God considers things like visitations, hearing His voice and moving in the power of God, as precious pearls. I knew in that moment that the only way we could receive the pearls (or precious things) of God was by allowing the Holy Spirit and God's fire to consume our hearts and birth purity. This purity is necessary for us to handle the precious things of God.

God's message to us as a body is that we need to become like the merchant in the Bible who gave his all to obtain the pearl of great price. Matthew 13:45-46 says, "Again, the kingdom of heaven is like a merchant seeking beautiful pearls, who, when he had found one pearl of great price, went and sold all that he had and bought it."

This was a significant message to me and to all of the churches that I preached at in that season. Through that angelic messenger, God gave us the direction and blueprint that would help us obtain another level of His presence and power.

Speaking of fire . . .

ANGELS OF FIRE

When I minister, I often see a vision of angels of fire. Once, in Redlands, California years ago, I stood on the stage of a church about to shift into some healing ministry. I suddenly experienced an open vision and saw angels flying around the room with coals of fire. When I experience an open vision, the entire room either fades into the background or disappears so that all I see is what God is showing me. That is what happened that night: the angels I saw looked just like those described in Isaiah 6:2. They had six wings; with two they flew, and with the other four they covered their eyes and feet.

The Bible calls them seraphim angels. These are angels who carry the fire of God's love. Their assignment from heaven is to help bring people into the purity and holiness of God, as well as prepare people's hearts to encounter God.

As I saw this I knew that God wanted to release freedom to the people that night and lead them into individual encounters with Himself. So I took the microphone and told this hungry group of worshiping Christians that God had sent his angels of fire, and that he was going to set people free from things that hindered them from coming into his presence. That night many people testified to experiencing the fire of God burning His love into them, setting them free from things that were strongholds in their lives; things hindering them from coming into the presence of God.

But the greatest thing happened right at the end of the meeting.

Just as we were about to bring the meeting to a close, I felt impressed to tell the hosting pastor that someone needed to give his life to Jesus. Right away, the pastor stood up and gave an alter call for salvation. Sure enough, a young man ran forward and gave his life to Christ! He testified that he had never felt God or been in a meeting like the one that night, and that he knew he had to give his life to Christ right then and there. He went from not knowing God to knowing God and finding out who he truly was—a son in his Father's kingdom!

This was similar to the journey of Isaiah the prophet. In Isaiah 6:6-8, Isaiah is commissioned as a prophet. His first visitation is a face-to-face encounter with God where he sees the Lord high and lifted up and sitting upon the throne. He hears the voice of the Lord speak and everything around him begins to shake by the reverberating power of God's voice. The temple in which he is standing is filled with the Shekinah glory cloud of God. Suddenly, Isaiah becomes aware of his humanity and realizes he is a sinful man.

He does what anyone would do—he freaks out! God helps him to get steady on his feet after a Seraphim angel uses tongs to pluck a coal of burning fire from the altar and places it upon Isaiah's lips. Isaiah is purged of his sinfulness and shortcomings, and is able to stand in the presence of Holy God.

> A single encounter with an angel of fire allows Isaiah to confidently stand in the presence of God, ready for action.

This act of the angel of fire enabled Isaiah to instantly overcome his fears and doubts, and releases a burning desire to fulfill his purpose on earth, enabling him to say, "Here am I God. Send me!"

During this encounter Isaiah discovers who God is and who he is. He discovers the majesty, power, and Holiness of God. A single encounter with an angel of fire allows Isaiah to confidently stand in the presence of God, ready for action.

This is what the angels of fire are sent to do: help those who feel disqualified or inadequate enter the presence of God and stand with confidence. God wants to send angels of fire to many of you reading this book, especially during your times of worship and prayer. He wants to shift your focus away from your shortcomings and desire to slink away from God, allowing you to refocus with confidence and expectancy upon Him. God wants to burn away all the things that hinder you from knowing Him more, and instead give you clear access to His presence and throne.

If there are things you are struggling with that are hindering you from worship—whether addiction, fear, worry, or depression—just ask God to give you an Isaiah-like encounter and watch what happens.

GUARDIAN ANGELS

Throughout time and history there has been much talk about guardian angels. One of the functions of the angelic is to look after humankind and to protect us from evil, or even death. In fact, this is a promise of God to you. Psalm 91:11-12 tells us that God has given the angels charge over humankind in order to keep us in all of our ways. It goes on to say that God's angels will bear you up and keep you from harm's way.

I remember the first time I ever encountered my guardian angel. Before I became a Christian I was a very mischievous kid. One night while my parents were out of town, I found the keys to my Dad's Corvette in his desk and decided to take his car for a joy ride. I'd never driven the Corvette before; I was only 16 and my Dad would not let me drive this particular car.

Where I grew up in Colorado forested land abounds; one forest stood about a mile from our house. Well, of course, I was not used to the power of the Corvette. I took off in the car and as I was coming around a corner I just totally gunned it toward that forest. It wasn't long before I completely lost control; the car spun out and flew off the road while I was going about 50 mph. I sailed into the woods and hit a bunch of trees.

I was not wearing a seatbelt, so when I hit the first tree I was ejected out of the driver's seat through the open top of the convertible.

Then I just rolled onto my back and watched the Corvette fly over me into the woods and take out a whole bunch of trees.

As I flew into the air, it was as if I was seeing it all in slow motion. I could see myself falling to the ground and it seemed like I was going to land on my head. Right before I hit the ground, however, I saw five flashes of light. It was like *Boom! Boom! Boom! Boom! Boom!* Five flashes of light! Then I just rolled onto my back and watched the Corvette fly over me into the woods and take out a whole bunch of trees.

I remember exactly when it happened, and how I had one very distinct thought: *Wow, God just sent angels to save me!*

I got up and ran all the way home. The only injury I suffered was a little scratch on my back that barely bled at all. It didn't even need any stitches. I am convinced that those five flashes of light were angels sent to save my life.

I'm sure there are times when you suspect you were saved by an angel or two. Why do you suppose that is? The role of guardians is to watch and guard you so that you can fulfill the time that is allotted for you on earth. What are you doing with your time? I believe that you were saved for a purpose.

After I was spared in the car accident, I began to realize I was not the only one who had experienced this kind of encounter. I found that many people, including leaders in the body of Christ, had been saved from dangerous situations just like mine. Look at this account of angels that came to the rescue for author and speaker Randy Alcorn when he was a teenager. Randy's testimony states:

> I'll never forget driving too fast as a teenager, looking down at something that distracted me, and then looking up to see all yellow in front of me. I swerved to the right, bumped along in a field, cut back onto the road and saw in my rear view mirror the school bus that had come to a complete stop in front of me. I knew immediately, the situation was impossible—I simply could not have been that close to the back of a school bus, where all I saw was yellow, going at that speed and not have crashed into it. Yet I didn't. God had graciously delivered me, and I suspect some day I'll find an angel or two were involved in the rescue.[2]

Not only do angels guard and have charge over adults, they also look after children. Jesus spoke about children having angels around them when he said, "Take heed that you do not despise one of these little ones, for I say to you that in heaven their angels always see the face of my Father who is in heaven" (Matthew 18:10).

I believe that this shows us that the Father in heaven *especially* watches over the children and even communicates with each angel regarding their child's welfare. Parents, you can rest assured that our Father in heaven is watching over your children and that He has their backs.

Parents, you can rest assured that our Father in heaven is watching over your children and that He has their backs.

HEALING ANGELS

One of the most common angels that show up as Miranda and I minister are angels of healing. An example of this kind of angel is found in John 5:1-4. Hundreds of blind, lame, crippled and sick people congregate each day at a pool called Bethesda, located near the sheep's gate of Jerusalem. They wait for an angel to come down from heaven to stir the waters of the pool. Whoever first enters the pool after the waters are stirred is instantly healed of their illness. They wait for a healing angel.

The first time I ever encountered a healing angel was during my teens. At that time I played baseball and was an up-and-coming pitcher, who was throwing and practicing way too much. One day, I threw out my arm; in fact, doctors told me it would be months before I could throw again.

My mom is a Christian and has always told me, "Pray to God." She believes in God's power and intervention. So I prayed, just asking God to heal me. I didn't really have a relationship with Him, but I said, "God, heal me." One night while sleeping I had a dream where I encountered an angel that came and touched my arm. When he touched my arm, I was instantly healed.

When I awoke, I realized that I had not just been healed in the dream, the healing manifested in my waking state. I had no more pain and no limitations in the movement of my arm. I was actually able to go out and pitch that weekend.

Years later, after I met the Lord and was launched into full-time ministry, I began to see many miracles as I preached. In fact, the anointing for miracles has really marked the ministry of both my wife Miranda and me. At times, when I stand up to minister, I shift into the revelatory atmosphere where I experience visions. When I see an angel come into the room and start healing people under the power of the Holy Spirit, I simply tell people in the room that God is releasing healing. It is not unusual to see twenty or thirty people healed in an instant—without either of us having to lay hands on them and pray.

Sometimes I tell people when I see angels, but most of the time I do not. In fact, I hardly ever tell people when I see a healing angel in the room because I want people to be focused upon Jesus, not on the angels of heaven.

During one particular meeting I declared to the 6,000 people in attendance that the healing power of God was moving in the room. That night, it seemed like hundreds of angels were moving among the crowd, setting people free from sickness and disease. As I became aware of heaven's activity in the room, I spoke out some ailments that I sensed the Holy Spirit was going to heal. I was pleasantly surprised afterward when more than 100 people came forward to testify of their miracles.

I will never forget the very first testimony given that night. A man had lost sight in one of his eyes as a 2-year-old after someone threw a stone at him. As we released the healing power of Jesus that night, the man could see perfectly out of his formerly blind eye for the first time since the accident!

At other times I have seen angels standing in certain spots in a room while I am ministering. When I see one stop next to a person, I simply ask God for words of knowledge of what he wants to heal, then call out the word, and ask the people near the angel if that word applies. Most of the time, one or more people in the vicinity of the angel are healed of whatever the Lord revealed.

If you need a miracle or prayer for healing and have no one available to pray for you, just ask God to send an angel of healing to minister His power into your life—and watch what happens!

WARRING ANGELS

The most classic scene in the Bible of warfare angels in action is in Daniel 10. Daniel is fasting and crying out for breakthrough for his generation. As he sets himself apart from others to hear the Lord more clearly, he ends up fasting for twenty-one days and nights. At the end of that time the angel Gabriel appears to him and tells him that the moment that Daniel's prayers left his lips, the Father in heaven answered his prayers. Gabriel goes on to tell Daniel that he would have come quicker but the prince of Persia had stood against him to resist him from coming. So God had to send Michael, a warring angel, to take the prince of Persia out so that the answer to prayer could safely reach Daniel (see Daniel 10:1-20).

Michael is an archangel and reveals that the function of warfare angels is to deal with the enemy's of God that resist His purposes in the spirit realm, so that His purposes will manifest in the natural. I am not talking about human resistance, but spiritual resistance. The Bible says that we wrestle not against flesh and blood but against powers and principalities and spiritual hosts of wickedness in heavenly places. (see Ephesians 6:12).

I encountered a warring angel one night while preaching at an amazing Russian-speaking church in Seattle where the glory of God showed up in a very special way. As I stood up to preach about the supernatural power of God, tiny feathers started appearing over peoples' heads. The manifestation of feathers continued all weekend. Over the course of three days, more than eighty angel feathers appeared. Everyone was shocked, yet excited at the same time, wondering what it all meant. I wondered, too and asked God to reveal the answer.

On the last night of the event I had a dream where God showed me what was going on with the feathers. I found myself inside this massive cave where I came face-to-face with a huge demonic being about the size of a ten-story building. I remember thinking, *wow this guy is big*, and started crying out for God's help. Instantly, two, large warrior angels appeared and started fighting this demonic being. As they wrestled, the whole earth began to shake. As they fought, angel feathers flew all over the cave. Finally, the two warring angels defeated the demonic creature and secured the victory.

After I awoke, I knew God had spoken to me about the meaning of the feathers that had fallen in the meetings: they where a direct result of warfare in the spiritual realm happening all around us during that particular set of meetings. The warring angels broke the power of the enemy and, as a result, many people received healing and were set free from things that were holding them back from God. Also, the atmosphere shifted enough so that we started making decrees and declarations over the city of Seattle, calling forth the purpose of God to release His kingdom power over that city so that many would come to Christ. After this experience, I realized that we Christians are more powerful in the spirit than we know.

One other amazing thing that happened that weekend involved the identification of the feather. The pastor was so excited about the feathers manifesting in the air that he took some of them to a well-known ornithologist who works for the University of Washington in Seattle. While delivering the feathers to the scientist he also picked a few pigeon feathers in a parking lot and asked his friend to examine both sets of feathers and tell him what kind of bird, or birds, the feathers belonged to.

> After this experience, I realized that we Christians are more powerful in the spirit than we know.

The ornithologist looked at the feathers and said he was perplexed. He was able to very quickly identify the pigeon feathers, but could not identify what species of bird the other feathers represented. My friend explained to the stumped scientist that they were angel feathers, which had appeared in his church that weekend.

The scientist replied, "Either you're telling the truth or you just discovered a new species of bird unknown to science before now." He went on to tell my friend that there are only two types of feathers when it comes to birds: One type is used for flying, and the other type for warming a bird in winter. "These feathers look like neither type. In fact, the feathers look like they were created to show off."

When he showed my friend the angel feathers under the magnification of the microscope, he could see the angel feather shone brilliant and strange oil seeped out of the fibers of the feather. I believe the scientist was viewing the anointing oil of God's glory radiating from the feather.

CHERUBIM ANGELS

Cherubim angels usher in the presence of God's glory, creating an atmosphere where signs and wonders can spontaneously bless those present. I have been blessed on many occasions when God opened my spiritual eyes to watch these angels help manifest His glory in dramatic ways.

During one meeting, the glory of God's presence came so powerfully that we felt the tangible weight of it during a time of praise and worship. Many people found themselves covered with gold dust, and many more received spontaneous miracles from God. Later, people reported being healed of deafness, back problems, damaged eye sight, as well as tumors and growths that were afflicting their bodies. This all happened after a time of worship to the Lord; and God responded by deploying the angelic realm into the meeting that day. The angelic presence of the cherubim shifted the atmosphere into a realm of signs and wonders.

On another occasion I saw a vision of a cherubim angel radiating the glory of God from his wings and body. As he showed up, the whole atmosphere of the room shifted and changed. When this happens, the miraculous follows and people get healed, delivered, and saved.

How do we know they are cherubim? Ezekiel 10:3-5 describes the realm that these angelic beings bring when they show up in our midst:

Now the cherubim were standing on the south side of the temple when the man went in, and the cloud filled the inner court. Then the glory of the LORD went up from the cherub, and paused over the threshold of the temple; and the house was filled with the cloud, and the court was full of the brightness of the LORD's glory. And the sound of the wings of the cherubim was heard even in the outer court, like the voice of Almighty God when He speaks.

As you read this passage you can see two things happen when these angels show up. They release the manifest presence of God in a tangible way and the voice of God is released, enabling all people in the vicinity to encounter God. As much as I love the signs and wonders realm of God's glory and presence, I love the latter part of this scripture even more. It says that those in the outer courts could hear the sound of God's voice when these angels were around.

> When angels show up one of the greatest things released is a level of revelation that enables people to have personal encounters with God.

When angels show up one of the greatest things released is a level of revelation that enables people to have personal encounters with God. We have had hundreds of testimonies over the last eight years where people testify of visions and encounters with Jesus, or angels in our meetings. I find that where the manifest presence of God is, there is access to visitations with Him.

Knowing what the Bible has to say about the different functions and purposes of angels can be very helpful in times of prayer. As I pray and get ready for a meeting I will often pray and ask God to release cherubim angels so people will have encounters with God and receive miracles from Him.

Sometimes its not how you pray but what you pray. Understanding what you ask for releases the manifestation of the things of heaven.

WATCHER ANGELS

Often times I will see watcher angels standing in a meeting just staring at the crowd, watching to see who is hungry for God. Usually when I see one of these angels they will be carrying with them a pen for writing and a pad of paper that looks like an ancient scroll.

I remember one of the first times I encountered one of these angels; it happened in an amazing open vision that occurred during a time of prayer. Jesus appeared to me, handed me a large torch of fire, and told me to preach about the fire of God's love.

As Jesus handed me the torch, I noticed an angel in the background staring right at me with a pen and a scroll in his hand. He was not just staring at my eyes, but instead seemed to be looking right at my chest. All of a sudden I had a funny feeling that the angel was not looking blankly through me, but that he was looking right at my heart.

After the encounter ended, I asked the Holy Spirit what the vision meant. I also specifically asked the Lord what the angel with the pen and scroll was all about. The Lord revealed that the angel I had seen was a watcher angel, and that one of the functions of the angelic, as outlined in Psalm 103:20, is to watch over the word of God in order to perform it.

Then the Lord explained the pen and scroll, revealing that one of the ways angels watch over the word of the Lord is to take note of the responses of men and women when they hear the Lord's word. When the angels of God see people responding in faith and hunger, they record the name of the person and report it to the Father. As a result, our Father in heaven releases a specific word over the individual's life.

I don't know about you, but I want to get heaven's attention.

The Lord also said that the angel I saw would begin traveling with me in order to watch the hearts of the people. Further, the angel would then record the names of those whose hearts responded in faith to the words I preached and prophesied, and that the promise of the Lord would be released to them.

Malachi 3:16-18 also reveals watcher angels in action. That verse talks about a group of people who got God's attention:

> Then those who feared the Lord spoke to one another, and the LORD listened and heard them; so a book of remembrance was written before Him, for those who fear the LORD and who meditate on His name.

I love this scripture passage! It says that God Himself listened in on the earthly conversations of a gathering of believers and liked what they were saying so much that He commanded a book of remembrance to be written, recording their conversation. I don't know about you, but I want to get heaven's attention.

Who do you think it was that wrote the things down that were pleasing the Father? I believe it was the work of watcher angels with their pens and scrolls! They were taking a log of the response of the hearts and words being said on earth so that heaven could have an account of the faithfulness of God's people.

When we are at church or in our homes praying, the angels of heaven are always watching our hearts. Those who pray in faith will receive the breakthroughs of God. You might be able to play church and fool men with all sorts of words and conversations, but God is always watching, and He will send his watcher angels into our realm to see whose hearts are truly hungry for His presence and love.

JOY ANGELS

When these angels are present, the manifestation of joy unspeakable shows up. Some religious people have a big problem with joy. They get bent out of shape because people sometimes laugh uncontrollably. The fruit of the encounter, however, speaks volumes about the authenticity of the angel of joy's work.

The Bible says that the angels of heaven rejoice when one person comes to salvation (see Luke 15:10). Salvation is a word that encompasses a lot more than going to heaven when you die. Being "saved" involves being healed, made complete and whole, and delivered. When angels of joy are present, they release the fullness of salvation—healing from emotional and physical disease and deliverance from harassing demons.

Joy angels also battle depression in many of my meetings. One of the keys to overcoming depression in the natural is through laughing; however, it can be very difficult for a clinically depressed person to laugh. I have been in many meetings were holy laughter breaks out. This type of laughter is different from normal laughter because the Holy Spirit, not man, initiates it. The Bible says that laughter does the body good like medicine (see Proverbs 17:22). When the angels release this realm of joy many people get healed and delivered by the power of God's spirit.

> This type of laughter is different from normal laughter because the Holy Spirit, not man, initiates it.

On many occasions, angels of joy entered the room and started messing with people, whacking them with the anointing of the Holy Spirit and joy. They are very playful in nature. They will run around the room and just grab people and often shake, poke or mess with them. As the angels play around and have fun with the individuals they are ministering to, the people often start laughing uncontrollably, getting set free from depression or even physically healed.

Several years ago, while conducting some revival meetings in England, God opened my spiritual eyes to see these angels in action. I remember one lady in particular who got touched by one of these joy angels. She fell off her seat in the front row of the meeting and began to laugh uncontrollably. Suddenly, her hat fell off. She was bald. After laughing for a while she came back to her natural senses, arranged her hat back onto her head and started screaming. She then stood and told everyone that she had came that night to the meeting believing for God to heal her of a massive cancerous tumor that was on her head. Apparently, during her laughing spell, God had healed her. She could no longer feel the tumor!

It was amazing! God had sent his angel to minister the joy of the Lord to this woman and it was like medicine to her body and the cancerous tumor totally disappeared!

The Bible is very clear that the joy of the Lord is our strength! When people are so down and out, or dealing with things like sickness, depression, or demonic attacks, God sends his joy angels to minister to them. What a wonderful God who enables us to laugh our way to breakthrough!

THE WORD OF THE LORD FOR YOU

Lord, open up my eyes to the angels that are found in Your word. Teach me, as I read Your word, how to recognize the angelic beings in the Bible when they are moving around me. Cause me to be aware of the reality of the angelic realm. In Jesus' name, I pray this. Amen!

4

HEAVENLY BEINGS & UNCOMMON ANGELS

L et's take a look at some of the less-talked-about angels in the Bible, such as the living creatures and the angels that appear as fiery horses and chariots. In this chapter I will also share a few testimonies of some more unusual types of angels that I (or friends of mine) have encountered.

LIVING CREATURES

In the previous chapter we discussed various forms of *typical* angelic beings in the Bible. In this chapter we're going to move on to more unusual heavenly creatures. First let's look at the living creatures, as talked about in Scripture. Revelation 4:6-11 is a great passage of scripture that mentions these heavenly beings known as living creatures. These amazing angelic beings hang out in (what I like to call) the "Throne Zone"—the area before the throne of God that's considered the sea of glass like crystal. Let's take a look at the portion of scripture that describes these living creatures so we can get a feel for what they look like and find out a bit about their roles in heaven:

> *And in front of the throne there was also what looked like a transparent glassy sea, as if of crystal. And around the throne, in the center at each side of the throne, were four living creatures (beings) who were full of eyes in front and behind [with intelligence as to what is before and at the rear of them]. The first living creature (being) was like a lion, the second living creature like an ox, the third living creature had the face of a man, and the fourth living creature [was] like a flying eagle. And the four living creatures, individually having six wings, were full of eyes all over and within [underneath their wings]; and day and night they never stop saying, Holy, holy, holy is the Lord God Almighty (Omnipotent), Who was and Who is and Who is to come. And whenever the living creatures offer glory and honor and thanksgiving to Him Who sits on the throne, Who lives forever and ever (through the eternities of the eternities), The twenty-four elders (the members of the heavenly Sanhedrin) fall prostrate before Him Who is sitting on the throne, and they worship Him Who lives forever and ever; and they throw down their crowns before the throne, crying out, Worthy are You, our Lord and God, to receive the glory and the honor and dominion, for You created all things; by Your will they were [brought into being] and were created. (Revelation 4:6-11 AMP)*

This passage of scripture highlights some interesting characteristics about these angelic beings. According to the Revelation of John, these creatures have six wings and both their bodies and their wings are covered with eyeballs in both the front and the back! That's pretty intriguing, if you ask me.

Firstly, let's look at the faces of the living creatures. Revelation tells us that there are four creatures that all have different types of faces. These faces include the face of a man, the face of a lion, the face of an ox and the face of a flying eagle. What is the meaning behind all of this?

> The book of Matthew has much more teaching on the kingdom of God and Christ's rule and reign than any of the other three gospels.

Many theologians believe that there is a face for each gospel in the New Testament and that each face represents a different aspect of the person of Jesus. It is believed that the face of the lion represents the book of Matthew and reveals Jesus as King. The book of Matthew has much more teaching on the kingdom of God and Christ's rule and reign than any of the other three gospels.

It is believed that the face of the ox represents the book of Mark and portrays Jesus as the servant of mankind. The face of the man represents the book of Luke and reveals the humanity of Jesus. Fourthly, the face of the eagle represents the book of John and reveals the prophetic aspect of Christ to the church.

Now let's talk about the eyes and wings on these heavenly beings. These fascinating creatures are covered with eyeballs all over their bodies, and including on both sides of their wings (see Revelation

4:8). I believe the reason that these creatures have so many eyeballs is because they may quite possibly be the watchers over what I call the "Throne Zone." They pay close attention to what is going on in Heaven and to what is going on before the throne of God at all times.

Worship is one of the key features of the living creatures. It seems that everywhere these amazing heavenly beings are found in the Scriptures, they are worshiping the Lord. I believe that one of the functions of these creatures is to lead the twenty-four elders in worship. As a result of the worship that is ushered in by these living creatures, the elders then cast their crowns down before God in praise and worship. Revelation 4:9-11 says:

> *Whenever the living creatures give glory and honor and thanks to Him who sits on the throne, who lives forever and ever, the twenty-four elders fall down before Him who sits on the throne and worship Him who lives forever and ever, and cast their crowns before the throne, saying:*
>
> *"You are worthy, O Lord,*
> *To receive glory and honor and power;*
> *For You created all things,*
> *And by Your will they exist and were created."*

This portion of scripture shows us that the living creatures love to give glory, honor and thanksgiving to the One who sits on the throne. Worship is pure adoration of the One who deserves it all—and these heavenly beings show us how it's done. The Bible says that day and night these beings cry out in worship to God and their worship triggers the twenty-four elders to praise God too (see Revelation 4:8-9).

CHARIOTS OF FIRE

One of the manifestations found several times in the Bible concerning various types of angels is the appearance of horsemen—and some of those angels manifesting alongside horses and/or chariots of fire. The Bible is very clear that this is what the young prophet Elisha saw when his spiritual father, Elijah, was taken up into heaven in a whirlwind. This experience happened right before Elisha received the double portion mantle:

> *And it came to pass, as they still went on, and talked, that, behold, there appeared a chariot of fire, and horses of fire, and parted them both asunder; and Elijah went up by a whirlwind into heaven. And Elisha saw it, and he cried, My father, my father, the chariot of Israel, and the horsemen thereof. And he saw him no more: and he took hold of his own clothes, and rent them in two pieces. He took up also the mantle of Elijah that fell from him, and went back, and stood by the bank of Jordan.* (2 Kings 2:11-13, KJV)

This portion of scripture clearly illustrates an amazing manifestation of the angelic host of heaven. In this passage, we can see that horses, chariots and horsemen of fire accompanied or represented the angelic. They came out of heaven to help transport Elijah safely to heaven, and in manifesting to Elijah and Elisha, made quite the impression. What is the purpose of this appearing and what is the function of this angelic representation?

Doesn't it make sense that heavenly horses and chariots would serve the same purpose as natural chariots and horses? In the natural, a horse and chariot would (in times of war) be used to move about swiftly so that one could advance or escape from his enemies quickly. In the same way, I believe that God uses his fiery chariots and horsemen so that the people of God can move around swiftly and advance kingdom mandates!

> Doesn't it make sense that heavenly horses and chariots would serve the same purpose as natural chariots and horses?

One of the ways angels move around is by instantaneously and supernaturally transporting from place to place. Though the Bible is clear that some angels do fly, there are many instances where they seem to just "appear." They oftentimes suddenly appear as a man (for example), and then just as quickly disappear to another place—no flying involved at all. This is supernatural transportation; it's one of the various ways that angels move around.

The prophet Elijah had a reputation of having strong angelic encounters and regularly being transported supernaturally. Could it be that these fiery angels (which appeared like chariots of fire) were the cause of Elijah's supernatural transportations? These transportations happened often and it would only make sense that his angels had something to do with it.

In 1 Kings 18:8-12 Elijah appears to one of Ahab's servants and gives him a message, requesting to meet with the king. King Ahab's servant says something very strange to Elijah as the prophet makes his request to see the king. Let's take a look at this conversation between the king's servant and Elijah:

And he answered him, "It is I. Go, tell your master, 'Elijah is here.'" So he said, "How have I sinned, that you are delivering your servant into the hand of Ahab, to kill me? As the Lord your God lives, there is no nation or kingdom where my master has not sent someone to hunt for you; and when they said, 'He is not here,' he took an oath from the kingdom or nation that they could not find you. And now you say, 'Go, tell your master, "Elijah is here!"' And it shall come to pass, as soon as I am gone from you, that the Spirit of the Lord will carry you to a place I do not know; so when I go and tell Ahab, and he cannot find you, he will kill me."
(1 Kings 18:8-12)

From this passage of scripture, we can see that Elijah had a special anointing of protection around him, and that he was transported many times. I believe that just like chariots and horsemen would have been the fastest and most effective modes of transportation or escape from danger for a king or important person in that time and day, it was a swift and supernatural way to transport God's servant out of danger.

Throughout Bible times, this type of heavenly transportation happened frequently. Elijah, Peter, Philip and even Jesus (just to name a few) were all supernaturally transported at some point or another. All of these amazing men of God were supernaturally transported from one geographical location to another for different kingdom purposes. For some, like Elijah, it was used as protection.

For others, like Jesus, God used supernatural transportation to make up time because of the work of the kingdom that needed to be done. Jesus walked on water to meet his disciples half way across the Sea of Galilee and then stepped into the boat with the disciples. But then, He and the disciples were immediately transported from the middle of the sea to land on the other side (see John 6:19-21).

Who knows? It is quite possible that if we were able to go back in time and see the angels of heaven that were around Jesus the night He walked on water and stepped into the boat with His disciples, we might be surprised to have seen the presence of the fiery chariots transporting them to the other side.

These types of angels are still active today: check out the following testimony of a man in Iowa who had an incredible encounter with a chariot of fire.

AN ENCOUNTER WITH THE CHARIOTS OF FIRE

Several years ago I was in Iowa speaking in several meetings, and the Lord had me preach on overcoming the fear of the supernatural. As the message came to an end one night, the Holy Spirit came upon me and I began to prophesy. I declared that God was going to release His wisdom and revelation and that He was going to push a religious spirit out of the region. The Lord further revealed that this ungodly spirit had been impeding people from fully entering into the deep things of God.

I prophesied that from that night on, there would be more supernatural experiences in that city than ever before, and that God would release Elijah-like experiences and encounters. Further, as a sign that this was the word of the Lord, many people and religious leaders in that region who had formerly opposed the supernatural would have Saul of Tarsus-like experiences. I finished the proclamation and then handed the microphone back to the pastor to close the meeting. At the time this was happening, a man and two friends who were driving toward the town had an amazing experience.

As their car approached the outskirts of town, two chariots of fire appeared in the natural to these men, right outside their car as they drove down the highway. There was a chariot on either side of the car and almost as soon as the men noticed the chariots, they fell into trance-like states.

When they came to their senses again, the car clock showed two minutes had passed from the time the encounter had happened. They then passed a landmark in the city that was *forty-two miles* away from the place where the chariots of fire first appeared to the men!

This was a completely supernatural occurrence. Not only was the open-eyed vision of the chariots supernatural, but also the time of the encounter versus the distance traveled was completely supernatural. The Lord gave these men an Elijah-like experience and transported them forty-two miles in two minutes. Why?

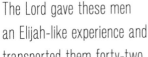

The Lord gave these men an Elijah-like experience and transported them forty-two miles in two minutes. Why?

The man driving the car showed up to my meeting the next night to testify about his unusual experience with God. This man's testimony confirmed the word that the Lord had spoken through me the night before regarding Elijah-like experiences happening to people in the region as a sign that the Lord was pushing back a religious spirit.

Afterward, the pastor of the church informed me that this man had been speaking against the things of the supernatural and a lot of things that this church experienced. The man's experience with the chariots of fire brought forth supernatural transportation, which in turn brought forth transformation in an individual's life.

A second function of these angels is to protect (or war) on behalf of God and His people. In 2 Kings 6, Elisha has an experience several years after his first encounter with these fiery beings, where he gets into a sticky situation and upsets the Syrian king. As a result of the king's anger, a massive army ends up on Elisha's doorstep (see 2 Kings 6:13-15).

When Elisha's servant sees this massive army outside of Elisha's home (in the natural), he panics and runs into Elisha's house to tell the prophet of their doom. It turns out that with one prayer, *everything* changes. Elisha prayed to the Lord for his servant to see in the spirit (see 2 Kings 6:17).

After Elisha prayed, the servant's spiritual eyes were opened and he saw those heavenly beings who were for them and not against them. Heaven's fiery chariots and horses were around them, and he realized there were more hosts of heaven with Elisha than those in the natural realm around them.

I believe the angels that looked like chariots of fire and horsemen were on assignment to protect God's prophet. I also think that if the natural armies would have attacked Elisha, the heavenly army would have either destroyed the king's men or supernaturally transported Elisha to a safe place. If this were the case, Elisha's testimony would have been the same as his spiritual father Elijah's (as we discussed earlier). Then the younger prophet would have become known as an untouchable prophet—one the Spirit of the Lord would have carried from one place to another just like with Elijah (see 1 Kings 18:12).

MARTYR ANGELS

Just recently, a good friend of mine who is extremely prophetic told me of an amazing encounter that he had with God while leading a mission's trip in Lima, Peru. His group held some amazing ministry events where God showed up big time! Many were getting healed, saved, and delivered.

One night after the meeting, the Holy Spirit spoke to my friend and told him not to go out to eat with the team. The Holy Spirit told him to go back to his hotel and wait on God. So he went to his room and started to wait on the Lord. After a few moments in prayer, the atmosphere of the room shifted and an angel appeared to my friend.

> After a few moments in prayer, the atmosphere of the room shifted and an angel appeared to my friend.

Instantly, the angel transported him to a massive field filled with angels sitting on horses. He asked, "Where am I?"

Then a man stepped out from behind the horses and replied, "Welcome to the field of martyrs." The man went on to tell my friend, "These are the martyr angels that are to be assigned to saints in the end-time army of God."

"Who are you?" asked my friend.

The man answered, "I am Stephen, and today God is assigning to you your martyr angel."

My friend was stunned.

"Don't be afraid. When it comes time for someone who is called to be martyred, the angels that you see before you will take that person's place and they will not feel any pain at all," the man explained.

The vision ended and my friend found himself transported back to his hotel room in Lima. Not only did he have an angelic encounter, but he had seen a cloud of witnesses and experienced them in the vision as well. Hebrews 12:1 speaks of a great cloud of heavenly witnesses who look down upon us to see what God is going to do in our time and day. They are cheering us on in heaven.

In this angelic encounter, God gave my friend revelation into the mystery of Stephen the Martyr's death. The angel was also named Stephen (but not the martyr Stephen himself, as angels are separate beings and not the souls of departed Christians); he told my friend not to worry about death as a martyr, because the martyr angel would take the place of the victim.

This makes sense and lines up with what happened to Stephen in the Bible. In fact, Acts 6:15 says that right before Stephen was stoned, his face shone like an angel. I believe that a martyr angel took Stephen's place and this explains why his face shone like an angel before his death. This also reveals the goodness of God in this type of situation.

God is so good that He will send an angel to take the place of a person experiencing martyrdom. There are accounts of Catholic saints in earlier centuries who, in the midst of persecution and impending martyrdom, cried out in faith, "Another lives within me and He will bear the pain!" Some died horrible deaths, yet their faces reflected only the peace and glory of God. Perhaps it was a martyr angel who took on the appearance of the person and bore the pain as God enabled the martyr to ascend to heaven.

FINANCIAL ANGELS

The first time I became aware of the fact that financial angels existed was when God started releasing visions of the treasury rooms of heaven to me. Financial angels respond to the Lord's direction to distribute funds where needed on earth.

The first time the Holy Spirit took me to the treasury rooms of heaven was in 2007. Since then, I have returned many times. The treasury rooms of heaven fill a massive storehouse that extends for miles and contains many chambers filled with gold, silver, and precious jewels.

The best way to describe this place is that it looks like the kind of treasury room that you would see in the movies, depicting the riches of a great pharaoh or king. But the reality is that this treasury room is ten times greater then any human could imagine. As I entered, I knew I was standing in the treasury room that belonged to the King of Kings and the

> God is so good that He will send an angel to take the place of a person experiencing martyrdom.

Lord of Lords. I also knew that this place was where the King of Glory stored up his treasures and released them to his children on the earth for kingdom purposes.

Some of you reading this right now may be asking where this is mentioned in the Bible. Matthew 6:19-21 was the scripture the Holy Spirit gave me after the first time I visited the treasury rooms of heaven, when I asked him that same question. Jesus mentions the treasury rooms of heaven when He says,

> *Do not lay up for yourselves treasures on earth, where moth and rust destroy and where thieves break in and steal; but lay up for yourselves treasures in heaven, where neither moth nor rust destroys and where thieves do not break in and steal. For where your treasure is, there your heart will be also.*

Some Christians are given the gift of giving; God gives these believers an anointing for creating wealth for the purpose of underwriting the work of God's Church on earth.

I believe that most importantly, this verse refers to spiritual treasure. In other words, that while the material treasures of this world always fade (e.g. monetary wealth, possessions, fame, and fortune), the immeasurable treasures of heaven never do (e.g. spiritual blessings and attributes). I also believe, however, that some Christians are given the gift of giving; God gives these believers an anointing for creating wealth for the purpose of underwriting the work of God's Church on earth.

When the Lord sends me to this place, an angel positioned to watch over the treasury rooms often escorts me around and shows me how God operates this amazing treasury system. One time I saw many angels going in and out of this massive room carrying gold and silver, along with precious stones. They released them to people on earth as they prayed, believing God for breakthrough in the financial realm.

I watched as these people began to receive strategies and even tangible finances in the natural, as heaven's angels released the treasures to them through visions and outright miraculous appearance of funds. For example, I know of debts being supernaturally canceled as a result of an individual's obedience to God to give to others, which in turn, released the financial angels to bless their own lives.

I also watched God give people instructions to test the obedience of their hearts. In one vision, I saw a woman crying out and asking God for finances for her rent. He told her to sow what little she did have into someone else and to trust Him. Then, as she was obedient to do what He asked, the financial angels were released to give her a portion of the treasures from the treasury room of heaven. The results were miraculous. She responded in faith to sow what she had and heaven released the funds she needed for herself.

The lives of those who followed the council of heaven tangibly manifested the treasures of heaven on earth because of the their obedience to the voice of God. In my experience, such financial encounters directly correlate to obedience and service, rather than with a person's earthly desires for wealth simply for wealth's sake.

I further believe there is a direct correlation between generosity and the release of finances from the treasury of heaven. One of the keys mentioned in Matthew 6:19-21 regarding receiving treasures and the release of finances is found in the last part of verse 21. After Jesus admonishes people to store up treasures in heaven, He says something very interesting: "For where your treasure is, there your heart will be also." Perhaps this is the reason why the people I saw in my encounters were having breakthroughs released from the treasury rooms of heaven: It was because of their willingness to be generous.

In being obedient to God's counsel they were showing God where their true treasure lay. It was in Him and His ability to take care of them. Their heart's focus on God and being generous brought down God's supernatural provision for them. They were sowing with their hearts not fixed on lack, but on God and his kingdom. And their faithfulness resulted in heaven invading earth.

A PRAYER FOR YOU

Lord, open my heart to know You more and open my eyes to see where You are. Like John, I want to see You as You are and be with You where You are. Please show me your glory! In Jesus' name, I pray. Amen!

5

AN ANGEL NAMED
PROMISE

Just recently I had an encounter with an angel named Promise. It happened one afternoon when I was praying in my living room in Pasadena, California. As I was praying, the atmosphere of the room changed and I went into an open vision where God began to speak to me about the promises of God.

When the atmosphere changed, my eyes were opened in the spirit and I saw a large angel that had a glorious cloud swirling around him. As I witnessed this supernatural occurrence, I realized the angel was staring right at me, and that he had a nametag on this chest.

It was the type of sticky nametag where you write your name in marker or pen following the words: "Hello. My name is…" and then stick it onto your shirt so others can get to know you. In my encounter, I noticed that the angel's nametag read "Promise."

Immediately after observing the angel and the swirling cloud around him, the vision ended. When I came out of the vision three things struck me: first, God had shown me this angel; second, the name of this angel was Promise; third (and most importantly), there was a glory cloud and manifest presence of God that was swirling around the angel.

As I prayed about this amazing encounter, the Lord told me He wanted to bring an increase of His presence, glory, and power to the earth. He showed me that many people around the world have been crying out to Him, asking Him for the next level of His presence and power. The Lord went on to tell me that one of the functions of angels is to oversee and release the promises of God over nations, regions and people.

> One of the functions of angels is to oversee and release the promises of God over nations, regions and people.

When the Holy Spirit showed me this, I realized that God wants His people to know He keeps track of His promises and is faithful to bring them to pass in the right time and season. This is especially true when it comes to the promises of God from within His Word. After this encounter I began to think about the word "promise," and when I did, I realized that some of Jesus' last words to His disciples before He ascended into Heaven were to "not depart from Jerusalem, but to wait for the Promise of the Father, 'which,' *He said,* 'you have heard from Me'" (see Acts 1:4).

In Luke 24:49 Jesus says, "I am going to send you what my Father has promised; but stay in the city until you have been clothed with power from on high" (NIV). This scripture gives us a clue about the promise of the Father. Jesus was prophesying about the baptism of the Holy Spirit and fire that would take place on the day of Pentecost not long after He would ascend into Heaven. The result of this prophecy is the church being endued with power from on high (see Acts 2:1-3).

After reading these scriptures and praying further about the purpose of the angel I saw, I felt the Lord tell me He was now releasing angels on assignment to cause revival activity to be stirred up in certain churches, cities and nations. These churches, cities and nations are ones that have believed God for the promise of a move of the Holy Spirit. As I thought about this, I began to realize that as a seer—or someone who has a gift to see in the Spirit—I had often seen angels stir up or shift the atmosphere of a meeting.

I recalled a time when I was in a large meeting and things felt quite dead in the spirit. All of a sudden I saw an angel come into the room during worship, and with that angel came the manifest presence of God. I have seen this many times over the last eight years of itinerate ministry, both in meetings in which I've preached, and in ones that I have attended. One thing I have noticed over the years is that whenever the glory of God comes into a room, so do the angels—they seem to work hand in hand. When the presence of God and the angels show up, miracles start to happen.

Not long ago I was preaching in a large prophetic conference at HRock, my home church in Pasadena, California. During my session of preaching, my spiritual eyes were opened and I noticed that a large angel had shown up while I was ministering. As soon as the angel had come into the room, the atmosphere shifted and it became charged with faith and expectancy.

Although most of the people in the room probably had no clue that the angel was there, he came to prepare the atmosphere for the miraculous. When I finished preaching my message, I sensed the Holy Spirit tell me to get the people to stand up and then release healing over them. In obedience to the Lord, I told the people that God wanted to heal people and that they should all stand up in the presence of God. I encouraged them to raise their hands if they needed healing in their bodies. I then began to pray and decree that the healing power of Jesus would be released into the room.

I called out words of knowledge and many were healed that afternoon. One lady came up to glorify God because she had been in a car accident where the vertebrae in her neck were so damaged that the doctors had to do surgery to allow the lady to hold up her head. The doctors had inserted metal pins to fuse her neck, which caused much pain, and she was in desperate need of a miracle. This lady testified that she was instantly healed in the atmosphere.

When I prayed for the healing power of Jesus to fall in the room, the woman felt her neck heat up and suddenly all of her movement and mobility came back. Since her surgery, she had been unable to look straight down or touch her chin to her chest because of the pins and rod that supported her neck. After she felt the fire of God's love touch her chest, she had full range of motion and could touch her chin to her chest for the first time. Praise God for this amazing creative miracle!

That same afternoon, approximately fifteen other people also testified to being healed from various ailments and injuries. These are the types of things that happen when the manifest presence of God comes, and when angels show up to accomplish their assignments.

I believe that God wants us to wait and pray with expectancy so we will be endued with power from on high, just as the early church was 2000 years ago. I encourage you to make time to pray and know that God sends his angels to release increased measures of godly presence and power.

LAKE'S PORTLAND ANGELIC VISITATION

John G. Lake, one of the most famous healing ministers of the 20th century, had an angelic visitation in his home in Portland, Oregon. During a time of prayer, an angel appeared to Lake in a vision and took out the Bible, opening it to the book of Acts. The angel called attention to the outpouring of the Holy Spirit on the day of Pentecost and then proceeded through the book, pointing out the great and outstanding revelations and phenomena in it.

Then the angel spoke these words: "This is Pentecost as God gave it through the heart of Jesus. Strive for this. Contend for this. Teach the people to pray for this. For this and this alone, will meet the necessity of the human heart, and this alone will have the power to overcome the forces of darkness."

> I believe that God wants us to wait and pray with expectancy so we will be endued with power from on high, just as the early church was 2000 years ago.

As the angel was departing, he said, "Pray, Pray, Pray. Teach the people to pray. Prayer and prayer alone, much prayer, persistent prayer is the door of entrance into the heart of God."[3]

I love this visitation of the Lord encountered by John G. Lake, where God showed Lake the key to walking in His fullness. As the angel departed from Lake's presence, he told the man of God that with much persistent prayer, the heart of God would be revealed to humankind. I believe God shared this message to teach the church how to position her to obtain the promises of the Father through the outpouring of the Holy Spirit.

A PRAYER FOR YOU

Lord, I ask you for the promise of the Father, that you would anoint me with the Holy Spirit and power. Send your angels on assignment to help bring the promises of God to pass in my life and in my family's lives as well, in Jesus' name. Amen.

6

GET READY FOR ANGELS TO TRANSFORM YOUR LIFE

A fast food Chinese restaurant became an unlikely meeting place between heaven and earth when I received a divine message one day. I had gone to our local Panda Express to eat lunch with a good friend. After ordering our food and sliding my tray up to the cashier to pay, the man behind the counter gave me a fortune cookie.

Immediately, I heard the Lord say, "Ask him for another cookie, I have a word for you."

So I asked the guy behind the counter if I could have another cookie, and to my surprise he did not want to give it to me. He said, "Only one per customer," but since the Lord had told me to ask, I was persistent. So I asked one more time, "Please, can I have another?"

Hesitating for a second, the man reluctantly gave me a second cookie by throwing it on my tray and giving me a dirty look. This didn't matter at all to me because I just wanted my prophetic word from God! My friend and I sat down to eat and I opened my cookie.

This is what it said: "A messenger will soon bring good tidings." I was shocked. It was like someone put a scripture in that cookie right out of the Bible.

Workout times are not really moments when you expect God to show up, but God is not confined to a church service.

Later that night I was upstairs in my room working out and praying in the spirit as I exercised. Workout times are not really moments when you expect God to show up, but God is not confined to a church service. In fact, I've been getting a little used to the odd times that spiritual encounters can occur.

As I was working out, the power of God came into the room (it's either that or I did one too many push-ups). Suddenly, I saw a flash out of the corner of my eye. As I turned to look, I saw an angel standing near me and then *boom!*—I fell flat on my face.

As the angel approached and stood over me, I noticed several things about him. First, he was wearing a crown containing a gem right in the middle. And the gem shifted colors—first red, then blue, then gold, and then repeated the colors.

As well, the angel had something in his hands—a long scepter or rod, the kind of that a king would carry. Just as I was looking at the scepter, the angel shoved it right into my belly. As he plunged it into me, I noticed that the head of the scepter was imprinted with the words "Jeremiah 1:9". At this point, the angel departed and I came out of the encounter.

After this experience, my stomach felt like I had done a thousand sit-ups! It was as if the moment when he shoved the scepter in my belly had to do with both conceiving something and of birthing.

I immediately opened my Bible to Jeremiah 1:9, which says:

Then the Lord put forth His hand and touched my mouth, and the Lord said to me, "Behold I have put my words in your mouth, see I have this day set you over the kingdoms, to root out and pull down, to destroy and to throw down, to build and to plant."

After I read the scripture, the Lord spoke to me and said, "Jerame, now is the time that I am going to put my word in your generation's mouth. I'm going to begin to give them an authority to be My voice in the nations. They will be those who will root out, pull down, and destroy the devil's kingdom. And they will effectively build, plant, and establish my kingdom rule and reign in the earth. And the way they are going to do it is through the color of the gems you saw on the angel's crown."

The Lord explained the meaning of the colors of the gemstones to me saying, "The red stone represents the manifold wisdom of God, the blue gem represents the revelation knowledge of Jesus as Lord and Savior, and the gold one represents the glory of God."

Then God said that as His people begin to speak out boldly what He said to them, He would release the manifold wisdom of God, (the red stone) which would root out, pull down, and destroy the powers, principalities and rulers of the air.

Once this was accomplished, God said He would release the blue stone, the revelation knowledge of Jesus Christ as Lord and Savior, in order to build a solid foundation for His kingdom. Finally, the glory of the Lord—represented by the gold stone—would be established in the earth and in the nations.

The number one reason why most Christians do not work with the angelic realm is because they are not aware of its function.

The Lord continued, "Jerame, I am about to raise up revivalists all over the world who are going to bring the gospel with authority and power, and they're going to take it to the nations."

The Lord continued, "Jerame, as a sign to you that this is the word of the Lord and my words to you are true, I am going to open up bigger doors for you to be a voice for me in the nations and to win souls. I am going to begin to give you a bigger platform in nations in this season. And this will be a sign to you that this is the word of the Lord for your generation."

The day after this encounter, I woke up and checked my voicemail, and on my phone was a message from a pastor at Toronto Airport Christian fellowship calling on behalf of John Arnott. (John Arnott pastored the church that hosted one of the largest revivals of the 20th century beginning in January 1994, known as the Toronto Blessing.)

They had called to see if I could take his place in a large crusade in Brazil that month. I called them back and was told that the crusade organizers were expecting between 5,000 and 7,000 people in these meetings. So within twenty-four hours of this angelic encounter, God confirmed the prophetic word that bigger platforms were indeed opening up for my generation.

You see, whenever we have encounters with the heavenly realm there should always be fruit that takes place. God immediately confirmed His word to me that this was a true word for our generation. I believe God is raising up an army to carry His voice in the earth right now. He is going to put His words in our mouths and His power in our hands. In fact, I believe that this generation that God is raising up is you. Its time to begin to seek the face of God and grab hold of the scepter of wisdom, revelation and glory that the Lord is releasing in this hour.

It is time for you to learn how to work with angels.

WORKING WITH THE ANGELS

God has assigned angels to watch over you and your life. The number one reason why most Christians do not work with the angelic realm is because they are not aware of its function. They are simply unaware that God has assigned angels to partner with them in releasing the things of the kingdom.

God wants to renew your mind and help you realize that He has placed heaven's helpers at your disposal, to accomplish His will on the earth. God wants to open your eyes to the world of the angelic so that you can be mindful of heaven's help all around you, every day.

WHAT MOVES THE ANGELS OF HEAVEN INTO ACTION?

The greatest thing you can do to align yourself with the angelic realm is to learn to hear the voice of God with clarity. Then, obey His voice and do exactly what He tells you to do. All of heaven's angels respond to God's voice and do what He says (see Psalm 103:20). Why shouldn't you?

When you are radically obedient to God, heaven breaks into your midst. While ministering to people on the streets, God has asked me to do some very strange and radical things. On one occasion I was eating in a restaurant when God told me to pray for three girls sitting nearby. As I prayed, the girls seemed to become overwhelmed by the power of God. As well, one of the girls noticed me being touched by God as I started to shake slightly. Actually, I started getting drunk in the Holy Spirit and one of the girls said, "What have you been drinking?"

I looked at her and said, "Nothing. It's the presence of God." Then I asked them if they wanted some of what I had. One of them said yes.

The Lord told me to wave my hand over the three girls, so out of obedience to His voice, I did what He said. As I did, one of the girls was visibly hit by the presence of God. Her friend, who obviously had been to church before, screamed out, "Run, he is releasing the fear of God!" All three girls bolted from the table and ran straight out of the restaurant as fast as they could. It was bizarre, but hilarious.

After that adventure the Lord explained that I had just partnered with the angelic to release the substance of His presence upon the girl who had been touched by His glory. That was the first time I became aware that God had assigned angels to my life, and that their purpose was to partner with me in releasing the things of God.

I asked the Holy Spirit to teach me more about how to partner with the angels of heaven. He said that because I was obedient in waving my hand over the girls, my obedience had released the substance of child-like faith. Then, when the angel assigned to me saw the substance of child-like faith, he reacted by releasing the substance of God's manifest presence.

I asked the Holy Spirit for a biblical reference, and He pointed me to Hebrews 11:1, which reads: "Now faith is the substance of things hoped for, the evidence of things not seen." As I read this scripture I began to understand a little bit more about the workings of the manifestations of the Holy Spirit. I discovered that when you pray for someone in faith, there is a substance that is released into the atmosphere of the unseen realm.

I had been in many charismatic meetings where people would pray for one another as they cried out for *fire* in Jesus' name, and the person who was being prayed for began to feel that fire. Hebrews 11:1 reveals that there is a substance to faith and that substance is connected to the unseen realm.

> When the angels of heaven see the substance of faith, they have no choice but to respond, as it is not a substance of the earth, but of heaven.

We humans may not be able to see that substance, but all of heaven and hell can. When the angels of heaven see the substance of faith, they have no choice but to respond, as it is not a substance of the earth, but of heaven. So when I release the substance of faith on a person who needs healing, it is usually because I first hear God specifically say to pray for that person or condition.

As we step out in faith and do what we are told by the voice of God, the angels see the substance of faith that is released. As we move, they respond by releasing miracle power over that person.

Now that you are aware that God has assigned angels to your life

> This generation doesn't just want to hear about God; rather, they want to have an experience with God.

to help you with what you are called to do, ask God how you can work with them to see breakthrough. After I discovered that I could work with my angels to minister to others, I began to have fun with it in church and on the streets. When I prayed for people to get healed on the street, I began to build an expectation for working with the angelic realm.

Right before I pray, I will say, "When I pray for you, you might feel fire or heat come onto your body." This sets the stage to work with the angels assigned to my life. I might pray something like, "Right now, in the name of Jesus, I command your back to be healed and I release the fire of God's love, in Jesus' name."

I find that as I pray this over the person, the angels of heaven release the fire of God upon the person. The person's faith explodes because they feel the fire, and they often experience the miraculous. Sometimes, even if the person does not receive a complete healing, he or she still accepts God's salvation because of feeling the tangible presence of God.

I believe such tangible expressions of God's love and power are some of the greatest witnesses of the reality of God to this generation. You see, we are living in a "show me" generation. This generation doesn't just want to hear about God; rather, they want to have an experience with God. So, if we as the church can learn to work with angels to release the manifest presence of God to those around us, we will see a massive harvest of souls enter the kingdom.

A PRAYER FOR YOU

Lord, help me to become aware of Heaven's help around me. Help me to see the opportunities and individuals around me where I can partner with the angels of Heaven to release Your manifest presence in those situations and on those people. I pray that You would continually use me to release Your love through signs, wonders, and miracles by releasing the substance of faith wherever I go. In Jesus' name I pray. Amen.

7

EMBRACE THE WINDS
OF CHANGE

Edmonton, Oklahoma was the scene of an extraordinary experience for my minister friend, Craig Kinsley and me. We had accepted an invitation to speak to a group of students at Central Oklahoma University. These were dedicated, Christ-loving students who had little exposure to anything beyond a conservative, non-charismatic tradition. In the religious Bible Belt of America, people are used to things being spirituality packaged in a correct, decent and orderly way, right?

The woman who invited us didn't mention that an evangelical church that had little experience with manifestations of the Holy Spirit was hosting the meetings. We expected it to be difficult.

The first night we got there I said, "Craig, you're preaching first."

He went out, preached, and it was really, really hard. No one seemed receptive. The next day was my day.

And so I'm lying on my bed in my room before the meeting, trying to soak in worship and prayer. *I need the word of the Lord for tonight for these young people*, I prayed.

As I'm soaking in prayer I kind of fall asleep. Then I realize that's not working, and decide to start praying in tongues. While I'm speaking in tongues, my voice starts giving out. I wasn't sure what to do, but knew that I needed to stop speaking out loud to save my voice.

So I seek God for further direction: *Lord, what do I have to do here to release breakthrough?*

And I hear the voice of the Lord say, "Why don't you spin around like a little kid?"

That's strange. But okay, why not? So I just start spinning around like a child. I spin for what seems to be a full five minutes, yet I don't get overly dizzy or nauseous. Then all of a sudden, as I'm spinning around, out of heaven, right in front of my face, this angel appears.

> All of a sudden he just disappears through the roof. And I'm left wondering if this just happened.

This is the most vivid angelic visitation I've ever had. This guy is huge, wearing a white garment with a golden sash, long hair, and a crown on his head that sported a red jewel. I stop spinning to stare at him. And he's just looking at me, glaring with arms folded across his chest.

I mean, I was lucky I didn't faint from fright right there. I thought, *What is this?* And then all of a sudden he just disappears through the roof. And I'm left wondering if this just happened.

Something catches my attention on the floor and as I look down I see a feather about four inches long, curled spirally, like a Christmas tree. I pick it up, and I look at it; then it dawns on me that my obedience pulled an encounter out of heaven.

The Lord says, "Jerame, if you'll be childlike, and do what I say when I say to do it, miraculous things will happen." He adds, "Unless you are converted and become as little children, you will by no means enter the kingdom of heaven" (see Matthew 18:3).

Immediately, I go next door and knock on Craig's room because I know he is inside, also praying. He opens the door and I hold up the feather and say, "Craig, look!"

He takes one look at the feather and grumbles, "That's not fair," then slams his door.

I can hear him in there saying, "God, I'm your son. I want a visitation too." And he starts pressing in, praying in tongues as I walk away.

I go back to my room and sit there stroking the feather; thanking God that He loves me. You know, when you have encounters with God, they're fun. So for a while I'm just rejoicing that the Lord visited me. Not long into my new prayer time, Craig comes into my room, looking shocked and amazed.

"That's the look, dude. You had something happen, didn't you?" I ask.

He nods his head and says, "While I was in there crying out, this angel came in. All I could see were the feathers spinning around, making kind of a whirring sound. And then he took this branding iron out and he branded my heart with the Song of Solomon." Craig, too, had this similar, supernatural encounter with God and I didn't even tell him that I had been spinning.

That is a night both Craig and I will never forget, that is for sure!

INTIMACY AND OBEDIENCE RELEASE HEAVEN

How was it that both Craig and I were favored with a divine encounter that night? Both of us had been in prayer, spending time with our Father, talking to Him, waiting for Him and expecting that since we are His sons, He would want to come and talk to us. That mutual conversation is called relationship. And the more time we spent relating to God, the closer, more intimate we become. Then, we learn to trust that God is speaking to us and it gets easier to step out in faith and obedience to do what we hear Him saying. Intimacy and obedience release heaven's intervention.

After we both had these encounters we did not know what to think about them. So what do sons do when they don't know what to do with visitations that God gives to them? I'll tell you what: they call their spiritual fathers. So that was exactly what I did. I called my spiritual father, prophet and speaker Bobby Conner, and told him all that happened, including the angelic visitations. He explained that it was the Angel of the Winds of Change that had visited both me and Craig.

God began to speak to me and give me keys to visitations with Him out of our experiences from that day. He said, "Jerame, you've got to hunger for me." He said, "Craig was desperate, and he made a demand. He saw that I visited you, and he made a demand because he's a son too, so I had to visit him."

When you have an encounter with the things of heaven coming to earth, God's presence increases. That night I went to the meeting and preached on the double portion of Elijah. The miracle power of God came into the room so heavily that it was palpable. Due to a terrible injury two years earlier, a female student had about thirty metal pins and seven metal plates holding her face together.

I received a word of knowledge and said, "There's somebody with metal in their body. Come forward." She came forward and when I prayed for her, God removed all the metal from her face. Then she testified that for the first time in two years, she could feel the sensation of touch on her face right there on the spot. Later on, her doctors confirmed that all the metal had disappeared and the bone structure had reformed.

As a result of that miracle, faith erupted and twenty other people were instantly healed. As the winds of change began to blow, revival broke out on this campus!

In one of the other meetings while Craig was preaching there were a couple of football players who had been injured and sitting out the season. They were instantly healed, crying like babies as God touched them. I came away

> As the winds of change began to blow, revival broke out on this campus!

renewed in my faith regarding angels and the miraculous, and began to see other similar instances.

Just prior to the writing of this book, I was in Scotland facilitating a set of revival meetings in a city called Broxburn, just outside of Edinburgh. On the final night of the meetings, I had an open vision of a mighty gust of wind blowing throughout the land of Scotland. I saw the angels of God releasing a swift wind that was blowing a dark cloud away from the nation and into the sea. As the angels blew the dark clouds out of Great Britain, God replaced them with a brilliant cloud of glory.

Meanwhile throughout the vision, I could still hear myself preaching to the Scots who were in attendance. When the vision was over, it was like *Wham!* I was back in my body, without having missed a beat in my message. When the night meeting drew toward a close, I felt the leading of the Holy Spirit to prophesy over the church and nation. God told me to open wide my mouth and begin to speak and that as I did, He would fill it with His word for the people.

The Lord told me to tell the pastor of the church that God was about to release the winds of change and blow the dark cloud of unbelief and insecurity out of the nation of Scotland so that revival could happen again. God also told me to tell the pastor that as a sign to him that this was the word of the Lord for his nation and church, there would be very strong winds in the natural that would show up after we left the city. I publicly declared to the pastor what the Lord had spoken to me and we ended the meeting shortly thereafter.

The next day my wife and I flew to Mannheim, Germany to minister in a conference there. Within three days, we received an email from the pastor in Scotland telling us that the word that I had prophesied to him had already come to pass.

He went on to say that a couple of days after we had left Scotland, a huge windstorm (which the media and newspapers dubbed the "storm of the century") had passed through their nation. The pastor explained that they had experienced gale-force winds clocked at 114 mph. The winds had blown so hard that they knocked down his family's backyard fence!

I believe that this natural sign resulted from a prophetic word from God, showing us that the angelic realm moves on our behalf. Also, I am certain that the angels were dealing with opposition that had been holding people back from hunger for revival and more of God's presence.

A month later the pastor hosted a unity meeting in his city to test the word. Prior to this "winds of change" sign, this particular church had trouble gathering people together for revival meetings. For some reason people seemed to be unwilling or resistant to come out to any church events, but after God released the winds of change, something shifted dramatically. The meeting ended up being the best-attended meeting that his church had hosted in years.

Many people who had never wanted to be a part of the pastor's meetings ended up coming out in healthy numbers. It was a true sign and confirmation that God had moved in Broxburn, Scotland. As in this testimony, one of the functions of the angels is to clear the atmosphere in regions, cities and nations of demonic influences that hinder the moving of the Holy Spirit.

As you can imagine, I was very happy for my pastor friend in Scotland when he told me of the fruit of this sign and wonder and prophetic word. He was excited because his region and nation had an encounter with the angel of the winds of change, which brought forth a positive shift in the spiritual climate—something well worth praising God for.

To follow up with this true story, we found out later that our pastor and spiritual father, Che Ahn, spoke in Edinburgh two months later, just 20 minutes from Broxburn. When he preached there, he witnessed some of the greatest miracles during his 20 years of ministering in Scotland. He believed that the angels of God had cleared the way for him to see the move of revival that he saw while in Edinburgh.

> The mark of a true encounter is revealed in the aftermath: when the winds blow, miracles increase and transformation happens.

The mark of a true encounter is revealed in the aftermath: when the winds blow, miracles increase and transformation happens. Embrace the winds of change. The winds of change are designed to bring revival to you—and through you.

THE WORD OF THE LORD FOR YOU:

Lord, help me to hunger and thirst for Your presence in order to know You more so that the realm of visitations opens up to me. Also, teach me to become radically obedient to Your voice so that heaven's helpers would work with me to demonstrate Your power to hurting people around me. In Jesus' name. Amen.

8

POSITION YOURSELF
FOR ENCOUNTERS

If we really understand that intimacy and obedience bring heaven to earth, I'm telling you things will happen. God may even give you authority over the weather. We've seen moments when God has given us authority over the natural elements, and it's always because we stepped out in faith and obedience.

A few years ago, Hurricane Ike started wreaking havoc in the Gulf of Mexico. We were scheduled to speak at a conference in Austin and the weather forecast reported that the eye of Ike was supposed to hit Austin during our Friday meetings. It was a serious time for Austin; people were packing up and evacuating. As Ike began to rage, the pastor called to ask whether or not I thought we should proceed with the meetings. I told him I would pray and get right back to him. As I prayed, I felt the Holy Spirit say, "Go, and everything will be all right."

I called the pastor and told him not to cancel the event; we were coming despite what the meteorologists said. So we flew to Austin on a Thursday night and went straight to the church to pray before the start of the meetings. As we prayed, I had an open vision of ninety-mile-an-hour winds being released from heaven and blowing Hurricane Ike to the east. I felt the Holy Spirit prompt me to decree this to happen in front of the pastors.

I prayed and declared that God would release the winds of heaven and the angels of God to push Ike to the east. That night when we all went to bed, a 90-mile-per-hour wind came out of nowhere and pushed Ike east, all the way to Galveston, Texas; we did not even get hit with a drop of rain in Austin. We were able to have the meetings and everything went great that weekend—except for the fact that we had really small crowds because most people had evacuated the city.

Because we had learned to see in the spirit and be obedient to God, this great miracle occurred. It happened as we proclaimed the word of the Lord to Hurricane Ike, and Ike responded. I believe that the angels of heaven were released to bring the winds as we spoke the word of the Lord, as we moved in faith and obedience to what God was saying to do. God wants to teach us how to position ourselves to have encounters with Him so we can walk in this kind of authority.

Positioning ourselves means that we spend time developing relationship with God, learning to hear His voice and enjoy His presence. Out of that position of relationship and intimacy, we gain authority—even over natural weather patterns. Out of our position of relationship, heaven and earth respond, releasing the angels of God to perform miracles as we decree what we hear the Father say. One of the most powerful ways He does that is by opening our spiritual eyes so we can see what He is doing in the spirit.

HOW TO POSITION YOURSELF FOR ENCOUNTERS

God wants to open your eyes to see in the spirit so that you can partner with Him to see heaven invade earth. He wants to open your eyes to visions, dreams, and even angelic visitations so you can decree what you see and change circumstances in peoples' lives, or even the destiny of the city or nation you live in.

> Even though Paul did not travel one day with Jesus, Paul accomplished more then any of the other apostles who had traveled with Him.

Paul the apostle is one of the best examples of a man who had powerful encounters with God. I believe we can learn how to engage in these encounters from looking at the example of his life, ministry, and writings. Paul was so different from all the other Apostles. He went from being the greatest enemy and threat to the early church, to the most powerful apostle over the early Church.

Even though Paul did not travel one day with Jesus, Paul accomplished more then any of the other apostles who had traveled with Him. He ended up planting more churches, leading more people to salvation, and writing more of the New Testament than any of the others.

What made Paul's testimony different was that God taught him by opening his spiritual eyes, and leading him through angelic visitations, dreams, visions, and revelation on the backside of the desert, away from all the others (see Galatians 1:11-12).

Paul was a "new breed" apostle who was taught by God Himself. Paul was fully led by supernatural encounters given by God, and had one of the most powerful prophetic ministries in the New Testament. In Ephesians 1:15-19, Paul even taught about how God wanted to open up the eyes of our spirit when he prayed that God the Father would give the people of that church a *spirit of wisdom and revelation* in the knowledge of Him. He also prayed that *the eyes of their understanding* would be opened that they might see into the spirit world.

I believe that this teaching gives us understanding of how to position ourselves to receive spiritual sight. Lets take a closer look at Ephesians 1:15-18:

> *Therefore I also, after I heard of your faith in the Lord Jesus and your love for all the saints, do not cease to give thanks for you, making mention of you in my prayers: that the God of our Lord Jesus Christ, the Father of glory, may give to you the spirit of wisdom and revelation in the knowledge of Him, the eyes of your understanding being enlightened; that you may know what is the hope of His calling, what are the riches of the glory of His inheritance in the saints.*

The first thing I want to point out about the spirit of wisdom and revelation is that God wants to anoint you so that you may know Him better. In Ephesians 1:17, Paul prays that the Father of glory would give unto the church (you and me) a *spirit of wisdom and revelation* in the knowledge of Him. You see—it's all about knowing Him. The number one reason why God wants to open up your eyes in the spirit and give you a spirit of wisdom and revelation is to encourage deeper relationship.

The Greek word for *knowledge* from the text above means "to know the precise and correct knowledge of who God is." You see, God the Father is raising up a Kingdom of sons and daughters who will know their Father in heaven, and out of that place of relational authority, they will administrate his kingdom on the earth.

Second, God wants to open your eyes to see in the spirit for the purpose of revealing to you your calling and destiny, as well as His future plans for His kingdom purposes in the earth. In this scripture, Paul is praying that the eyes of our understanding would be enlightened so that we would know the hope of Jesus' calling, and His inheritance in the saints. You see, when we as a church begin to see Jesus' calling, and the purpose for which He came, we begin to understand *our* calling and the purpose for which we are here.

> The number one reason why God wants to open up your eyes in the spirit and give you a spirit of wisdom and revelation is to encourage deeper relationship.

In the Greek, that phrase to have *the eyes of your understanding being enlightened* means to have the eyes of our hearts flooded with revelatory light. When you begin to tap into the spirit of wisdom and revelation, and the eyes of your heart begin to flood with revelatory light, you will begin to have angelic encounters as well as dreams, visions, and other supernatural experiences with God. These revelatory experiences are given in order to reveal to you the plans of God in the earth.

God sent Jesus as a model for us to know how we should walk as the sons and daughters of the Most High God. Jesus never did a thing unless He first saw what His Father in heaven was doing (see John 5:19). God clearly wants us to see and understand the calling of Jesus; because when we do, we know who we are, and when we can clearly see what our Papa is doing, we can do great exploits for Him.

> God sent Jesus as a model for us to know how we should walk as the sons and daughters of the Most High God.

After God began to open this revelation up to me, I began to make this portion of scripture personal, applying it to myself in prayer. I believe that there is power in praying scripture. We need to begin to pray Ephesians 1:15-18 over ourselves. I just began to pray that scripture, and put my name in it, praying something like this:

> "Lord, I am asking you to give me a Spirit of Wisdom. Give me a Spirit of Wisdom and Revelation in the knowledge of you. Open up my sense of sight, and enlighten the eyes of my heart, God, that I might know Your calling in my life, that I might know the inheritance that You have for your son and for me."

I began to pray that every night before I went to sleep, and you know what happened? I began having dreams, visions, and encounters with God.

It wasn't a repetitious-religious thing to me, such as praying the same thing over and over again. I meant it with all my heart when I prayed this to God. What I was really saying was, "God, I really want to know You."

Praying the Word of His promise means that we need to understand the Word. One of the greatest things we can do to boost our spiritual sight is to read the Word. The Word of God will bring an impartation or framework to you so you can see. I encourage you to read Revelation chapters 4 and 5 over and over again, and ask God to open your sense of sight, and to release to you the spirit of wisdom and revelation, and watch what happens.

When I first started really seeing angels in the spirit, the Lord challenged me to read the Word. God kept telling me, "Son, if you want to see the angelic, then study about the angels in the Bible." So, I started to look up every story about the angelic realm I could find in the book.

> God wants to open up your eyes so He can show you what His game plan is for your life and ministry.

I began to realize that some portions of scripture contained many descriptions of what angels looked like and I began to learn, by the word of God, what their functions were.

When God begins to show you things in the spirit, it's always for a purpose. I believe that God wants to open up your eyes so He can show you what His game plan is for your life and ministry. Often times in our healing meetings I will see the angelic beings come into the meetings like shafts of light. Usually, when I see these beings,

I ask God for words of knowledge for healing, and then ask people to stand—and typically they are located right in the spots where I see the shafts of light. Most of the time people get healed.

God wants us to be aware of what He wants to do in a city, state, region, or household. Sometimes, He will give us simple direction through a dream or vision to make a decree, or pray about that direction, and the results are huge when we follow through.

Obedience manifests the kingdom. God is going to raise up a generation that moves in obedience just like Elijah, to do the same for the glory of God. Elijah walked in authority and power that was even demonstrated over the natural elements of the earth, when he prophesied to king Ahab that there would be no rain except by his word. God is restoring the true prophetic authority to His church, so that when we speak the word of God it comes to pass.

CONFIDENCE INCREASES
WHEN YOU SEE THE ANGELS

Another reason why God wants to open up your "sense of sight" is because He wants to increase your confidence in Him. Something happens when you know who is *for* you rather then just who is *against* you.

I have been in many meetings in third world nations were it is not safe to preach the gospel. We have been through war zones and places were it's illegal to preach, places were people are being killed daily.

Just recently we were in a very dangerous city in Peru to conduct an evangelistic crusade. Our host contact brought to my attention just how dangerous it was for us to be in that place preaching. They told me our crusade was set up right in the middle of an area that was known as one of the most violent gang areas of Peru. They told us to make sure we kept a good watch on our team as a safety precaution.

As the worship took place, God opened my spiritual sense of sight and I saw a huge angel of pure white light, the size of a two-story building, appear right above the platform. Suddenly, I was filled with boldness because I knew God was showing me that I didn't need to worry at all—heaven was backing me up. As God spoke this to me, I got up and spoke with supernatural boldness and power; many gave their lives to Jesus that night, and many radical miracles happened.

THE TESTIMONY OF JESUS AND THE SPIRIT OF PROPHESY

Another key to having spiritual experiences is to get into the presence of others who experience supernatural encounters with God.

I remember early in my walk with the Lord, I had an encounter that changed everything for me. At the time I was living in Abbotsford, British Columbia, and was hanging out with a friend who had had way more experience with the supernatural than me. At this point in my life, I had not had any angelic encounters and was desperate to encounter God. So I prayed for the supernatural gifts of God's Spirit to be activated in my life daily.

My friend told me a story about a time an angel imparted a gift to him. When the angel appeared, the angel was holding something in its hand. Then the angel walked up to him and shoved it into his belly. Afterward, the Holy Spirit revealed that a gift of revelation was imparted to my friend that day.

Sure enough, my friend began having visionary experiences with God. After he told me about this encounter, he went on to prophesy over me about how God wanted to encounter me like He did with him. He told me to expect to receive an encounter soon.

So I went home and was super excited to press into the Lord. That night, I began to press in through worship and prayer, but nothing really significant happened. The next day at around 6:30 a.m., I got up to pray again. I began to pray in tongues, and in a mater of a few minutes I fell into a trance and entered into an encounter with the Lord. Everything went blank—but all of a sudden I could sense an angel in the room. I then felt a hand go into my belly and the presence of God was overwhelming.

I came out of the trance and began to ask God about the meaning of the experience. The Lord told me that He had just sent an angel to impart to me a gift to see in the spirit. I was excited! Just like my friend had prophesied, I had received an encounter with an angel, and God had given me a gift of revelation, too.

We need to surround ourselves with people who are full of faith, who are living in the supernatural daily. We need to learn to value the supernatural testimonies we hear from others so we can step into the same kinds of encounters in which they are walking. If you can't find people who are moving and living in the supernatural in your church, town or city, then obtain some books and teachings from others who are moving in the supernatural.

You can find this principle in Revelation 1:9. This scripture says that the testimony of Jesus is the *spirit of prophecy*. This means that when we talk about the supernatural, we actually activate it in our lives and the lives of those around us. You can see this in action in the life and ministry of Jesus as He transfers the anointing to His disciples.

As they hang out with him, they begin to be activated in the supernatural. Sometimes the anointing of God is more caught then taught. If you could catch a cold from someone who is sick, how much more can you catch the anointing from someone who is on fire for God? Jesus' disciples followed him around and watched Him do the stuff, and ended up working miracles on their own.

When I heard the testimony about my friend's angelic encounter, the Spirit of God used that testimony to activate me into my own encounters. We have seen this happen to hundreds of people who have attended our meetings. It is not unusual for us to get several emails after we speak in a city or nation where people let us know that they were activated into the seer realm after hearing us talk about angels.

> We need to surround ourselves with people who are full of faith, who are living in the supernatural daily.

I remember one specific testimony of a pastor's son who was from the Gold Coast of Australia. This young man had never seen in the Spirit. One of his greatest desires was to have visions and to see the angels of heaven. When he found out that we were coming to speak at his church, he made sure to come to the meeting with expectancy in his heart, believing that he would get activated in the seer realm.

My message to his church was about the fire of God. I even told a specific testimony about a time when an angel of fire had visited me. As I told the testimony of my angelic encounter, God opened the pastor's son's spiritual eyes, and for the first time ever he saw the angels of heaven. The young man suddenly saw not one, but *five* angels of fire standing behind me as I ministered.

> God speaks to me through the still, small voice more than He speaks to me through angels and supernatural visions and dreams.

I will never forget his excitement when he met me in the back office of the church after the meeting. With much enthusiasm, he told me that while I spoke about seeing the angel of fire, he asked God to open his eyes—and it happened! He came into faith because of the testimony and *boom*, his eyes opened. The key to this man's activation was that he came in expectancy to be activated, and then he asked God that my testimony would become his also. This key launched the young man into a visionary gift of his own.

HOW GOD SPEAKS TO ME

God speaks to me through the still, small voice more than He speaks to me through angels and supernatural visions and dreams. He speaks to me through His Word and by His Spirit. I'll just be waiting on the Lord before a meeting and He speaks quietly. Often I will pray in tongues, or I'll sit with my eyes closed; and to be honest, most of the time I never seek anything angelic. I just worship Jesus.

I tell you, I am just all about the presence of God. So, I'll start off my prayer time just saying, "Holy Spirit, I love you. I want to be with You. And in the midst of me being with You, I make myself available to You right now. If You want to show me something, if you want to speak to me, here I am." And I worship and praise.

I find that when I position myself simply, with worship and praise, that place in His presence opens up revelation and encounters. Mind you, there doesn't always have to be an "experience" where something happens; most of the time I don't have dramatic encounters like I've described above. However, significant encounters of breakthrough during meetings always begin with prayer.

The Bible reveals so many different ways that God speaks to His children. Whether it's through a quiet knowing in your mind and heart, or through a prophetic word, or angelic encounters, it is always for the same purpose—to release the purposes, plans and pursuits of Father God.

John 10 is a wonderful chapter that reassures us that we are Christ's own, and that He hears us. John 10:14-15 says, "I am the good shepherd; and I know My sheep, and am known by My own. As the Father knows Me, even so I know the Father; and I lay down My life for the sheep." Further on, in verses 27-28, Christ assures us by saying, "My sheep listen to

> Significant encounters of breakthrough during meetings always begin with prayer.

my voice; I know them, and they follow me. I give them eternal life, and they shall never perish; no one will snatch them out of my hand" (NIV). How wonderful to know that Jesus hears our voice when we speak to Him, and that we can hear His as well!

Angels are messengers from heaven, so they bring the purposes, plans and pursuits of God to be released in the earth. Often times when I minister in a city or nation, God gives me an angelic encounter or vision to show me the specific breakthrough that He wants to bring to that region or specific group of people. God does it to reveal to me what He wants to release so that I can then preach on it.

> Too much Spirit and not enough Word, and you're just flaky. Too much Word and not enough Spirit, and there's legalism with no power to it.

For example, if I have an angelic encounter and the angel tells me that God is bringing freedom, I will preach on "wherever the spirit of the Lord is, there is freedom" (see 2 Corinthians 3:17, NLT). In preparing for the message, I go through the Bible and find everything about how Jesus set the captives free and opened up prison doors.

To me, the Word and the Spirit go hand-in-hand. If you have too much without the other, you're out of balance. Too much Spirit and not enough Word, and you're just flaky. Too much Word and not enough Spirit, and there's legalism with no power to it. I believe there has to be balance of Spirit and Word. And I have been so blessed by how God does this with me. He gives me spiritual encounters; that is, He leads me by the Spirit, I preach on it from the Word, and we see significant breakthroughs!

HOW DO I KNOW IF I'VE SEEN A REAL ANGEL?

One of the most frequently asked questions I get regarding the angelic realm has to do with what angels look like. This is a good question. One thing is for sure: they are not fat little babies riding around on clouds with harps and bows and arrows.

I have seen many different types of angels—large angels, small angels, different colored angels, male-looking angels, female-looking angels, angels with wings, and angels with no wings. Heaven is full of creative beings. God created scores of angels and not one of them looks alike. Just like we are created individually and uniquely, so are the angels of God.

There are other times where I have not seen the figure of an angel but the angels appeared like flashes of light.

Most of the time, however, the angels I see fit the descriptions you read about in the Bible. You can discover a lot about angels by studying the word of God. It gives many examples of what the angels of heaven look like and what they do.

Now I would like to tackle a more controversial topic. Many people, including myself, have had encounters with angels that took on the appearance of either a man or a woman. I would like to bring some clarity to this subject instead of simply avoiding the topic. The Bible is very clear that angels are neither male nor female.

Further, God's word says that only humankind is made in God's image. The very first chapter of the Bible says pointedly that man is made in God's image:

> Then God said, "Let Us make man in Our image, accord-
> ing to Our likeness; let them have dominion over the fish of

the sea, over the birds of the air, and over the cattle, over all the earth and over every creeping thing that creeps on the earth" (Genesis 1:26).

Nowhere in God's Word does he say he made the angels in His image—only humankind. Though entire books of theology have been written on the subject of what it means to be made "in God's image," most biblical experts agree that only humans—and not angels—are made in His image (e.g. likeness, identity, characteristics, etc.).

I believe the angels' appearance is more metaphorical than literal. I don't think appearance is necessarily about gender as much as it is about what those features represent. In other words, a male-looking angel represents a more masculine aspect of God. You will see this with warring angels like I talked about earlier. As I have seen these angels they tend to be huge, muscular and full of power. Most of the time they have the appearance of strong-looking men.

> I believe the angels' appearance is more metaphorical than literal. I don't think appearance is necessarily about gender as much as it is about what those features represent.

On the other hand, I have also had visitations of angels that took on more feminine features. Feminine-looking angels focus on the wisdom of God, or revelation. The reason why I believe this is true is because the book of Proverbs talks about wisdom as a *she* (see Proverb 1:20). I believe that when an angel appears to someone in female-like form, it's a metaphorical sign that an angel is releasing the wisdom of God to the person having the encounter.

Often an angelic visitation is not about what the angel looks like as much as it is about the message it brings to me from the Father. Sometimes I will have encounters with angels that have objects in their hands, or they might be wearing an interesting garment or adornment. Pay attention to the small things in an encounter, as well as the big things. Sometimes the visitations we have are more metaphorical than we realize.

> Often an angelic visitation is not about what the angel looks like as much as it is about the message it brings.

You will need to pray about the meaning of the visitation to get the full understanding. For example, I was attending a meeting where the speaker asked people to close their eyes and pray because the Holy Spirit wanted to reveal some nations they were called to pray for that evening.

I closed my eyes and saw an angel standing in front of me who looked Asian. He wore a traditional garment, which I noticed had the Korean flag on it. The angel presented me with a large sword, which had a scripture written upon it: Hebrews 4:12. Then, just as fast as the visitation happened, the angel vanished.

This encounter was more metaphorical then traditional. Traditionally, you read about angels talking to people and giving them a message. In this encounter the angel did not say anything to me. He just appeared as an Asian man and handed me a sword with Hebrews 4:12 written upon it.

Hebrews 4:12 says, "For the word of God is living and powerful, and sharper than any two-edged sword, piercing even to the division of soul and spirit, and of joints and marrow, and is a discerner of the thoughts and intents of the heart." I knew that this encounter was actually God commissioning me to bring the prophetic word of the Lord to the nation of Korea.

Afterward, I realized that I needed to focus more attention on the nation of Korea in prayer as well as in my ministry schedule. I had already ministered in Korea several times, and I knew that God would open up more doors in the near future. But what a way to reveal it to me!

Sometimes angels will speak a message to you; and other times, you will have to pay attention to what the angel looks like, what it is wearing, or what it is doing. Sometimes I see angels performing certain actions like dancing or praising God. When I see them dancing, I know it is a good time to move the meeting into praise and worship. When I see angels just standing behind someone or pointing at the person, I know that God is highlighting a person to prophesy over or pray for.

Remember, the angels of heaven are sent to assist us in ministry and what we are called to do (see Hebrews 1:14). After every visitation, we must go to the Holy Spirit in prayer and ask God what the encounter means. If we do, He is faithful to give us understanding of the visitations we have. If you don't figure it out on your own in prayer, ask a friend who is also prophetic or a pastor or leader. In the multitude of many counselors there is wisdom (see Proverbs 11:14, 15:22).

THE FRUIT OF AN ENCOUNTER WITH GOD

Once you have discerned the reason why an angel visited you and the meaning of what was imparted through that encounter, some breakthrough must occur either in your life or ministry. If you really experienced a face-to-face encounter with God through an angelic visitation, vision or dream, it must bear the fruit of a genuine encounter with God.

Too often, people claim to have encounters with God but refuse to live a lifestyle set apart from the spirit of this age. A genuine visitation increases the

> Too often, people claim to have encounters with God but refuse to live a lifestyle set apart from the spirit of this age.

presence of the Holy Spirit in our lives. We become more heavenly minded and focused if we experience a true encounter.

This is not to say that we won't have strange or weird encounters with God though.

The Bible is full of strange and weird encounters. Just take Ezekiel for example. In Ezekiel 3 God appeared to the prophet with a scroll and told Ezekiel to eat it. He does, and it is sweet like honey in his mouth and bitter in his stomach. That is a weird encounter.

None of us, if we wrote the script of the Bible, would have thought of making someone eat a big piece of paper signifying the commission of a prophetic office, but that's what God did. God will often offend your natural thinking to reveal your heart. If the visitation lines up with the nature and character of God and produces that character in you, it is likely an authentic encounter.

The best thing you can do after an encounter with God's "kingdom come" is write it down, then go back to God in prayer and ask Him specific questions. Spend time cultivating a listening ear tuned into the way He speaks to you, personally. As well, seek wisdom from your spiritual covering, and submit yourself to their counsel.

If you want to know if a visitation is from God and is real, ask these three questions:

1. Does the spiritual encounter produce the fruit of the Holy Spirit in my life and leave a genuine hunger for more of Him afterward?

2. Does the encounter lead me or other people that much closer to God?

3. Does the encounter line up with the Word of God and produce a change in my life according to the revelation I receive?

I believe that if we ask these three things we will know quickly if a visitation we have is genuine or not. Also, another fruit of an encounter with God is that it will release a sense of God's calling or destiny to a believer. As well, the encounter will at times open up the favor of God in a person's life to step into their destiny and callings.

MARIA WOODWORTH-ETTER

Many people throughout time and history have had significant angelic visitations that revealed to them their callings and gave them vision for their lives and destinies. After these angelic visitations, these people received the faith to go for the seemingly impossible. And the fruit of their experiences still remains today.

Nineteenth century minister and prophetess Maria Woodworth-Etter is a great example of someone who moved powerfully in angelic visitations and miracles. Her first real significant visitation of God happened well before she was ever in ministry. One night when Maria was praying to God, the angels of heaven came into her room. The angels took her in a vision to the West, over prairies, lakes, forests and rivers and then to a long, wide field of waving golden grain. As the vision unfolded, she began to preach, watching as the grain began to fall like sheaves.

Before this encounter, Maria was a stay-at-home mother and wife. Shortly after this angelic visitation, however, she was launched into full-time ministry and has been called the grandmother of Pentecostal Christianity. Maria Woodworth-Etter was a powerful preacher who saw thousands come to Christ and many get healed and delivered in her meetings.[4]

Maria ministered in the late 1800s and into the early 1920s and had a powerful ministry of signs, wonders and miracles. Her angelic visitation gave Maria the faith to believe God that she could preach the gospel in a man's world, during a time when women preachers were not accepted in normal church society.

THE WORD OF THE LORD FOR YOU:

Lord, I ask you for the Spirit of Wisdom and Revelation in the knowledge of you, and I ask that you would open the eyes of my heart and flood them with revelatory light that I might know you more. Open my eyes to see into the spirit realm and give me dreams, visions, and

angelic encounters, in Jesus' name. Amen!

9

ANGELIC ATTRACTION

Now that we know how to position ourselves for encounters with God and have the tools necessary to discern between a godly visitation and a false one, lets look at what attracts the angels of heaven to a believer.

WORSHIP ATTRACTS ANGELS AND BRINGS BREAKTHROUGH

A few years ago while in Santa Rosa, California the Lord began to show me the power of praise and worship, and how it attracts heaven's attention to bring heaven's help. Many times in worship services I have seen angels appear to worship alongside the people of God.

During this time in Santa Rosa, we were doing revival meetings in the Wells Fargo Convention Center on the outskirts of the city. My job that night was to transition the meeting, greet the people, and introduce the main speaker. As I got up to transition the meeting from the time of worship to the speaking aspect of the session, I noticed that the people were really connecting with God in a pure realm of worship.

As I watched people lifting their hands in worship and singing passionately to Jesus, my spiritual eyes began to open. As they did, I saw a large angel—about twenty feet tall—walk into the room. I noticed he had a large set of keys in one hand and an old-time looking chain and shackle in the other. I knew the moment that I saw this that the keys were to unlock the prison doors and break the

> I asked the Holy Spirit what to do, and I sensed Him say, "Have the people worship a little longer; I am releasing freedom into the room."

shackles of sin and bondage that were holding people back from God in that very room.

I asked the Holy Spirit what to do, and I sensed Him say, "Have the people worship a little longer; I am releasing freedom into the room." So I did as I was told and I watched as this large angel begin to minister to people. As I watched the angel move, I knew that he was breaking the chains of bondage and sin from people's lives and that those whom the devil had bound were being set free.

After watching this happen for a while, the Holy Spirit told me to get up and tell the people that it was going to be a night of Acts 16:25-26. He told me to tell the people that if they would just keep worshiping the Lord, He would break the chains off their lives and open the prison doors of bondage.

As I announced this, I knew that for many that night the struggle would soon be over because God was destroying the strongholds of the enemy over their lives. The key to their breakthrough, however, was the same key that Paul and Silas discovered while in prison in Acts 16:25-26, which says,

> Around midnight Paul and Silas were praying and sing-
> ing hymns to God, and the other prisoners were listening.
> Suddenly, there was a massive earthquake, and the prison
> was shaken to its foundations. All the doors immediately
> flew open, and the chains of every prisoner fell off! (Acts
> 16:25-26, NLT)

I knew that as we praised (just like Paul and Silas had), a shaking was taking place in the realm of the spirit that was setting free all who were oppressed. My eyes were opened in the spirit and I could see chains breaking as we kept praying and praising.

Later that night, many came forward to testify of their great breakthroughs over depression and oppression. Because of what happened in the realm of praise that night, many were set free from addictions and bondages such as pornography, fear and anger. All of this happened when we lifted up our voices and praised in the manner of Paul and Silas.

This encounter taught me that worship and praise cause heaven's help to be attracted to us and when these angelic helpers show up, powerful things happen.

> Don't focus on the angels, but focus on the King of the kingdom, Jesus Christ!

Don't focus on the angels, but focus on the King of the kingdom, Jesus Christ! As you do, all of heaven will be attracted to you and God's healing, and delivering power will come crashing into your midst. Therefore, if you want to attract the angelic realm, worship Jesus with all of your heart; heaven's help will come as a result.

INTERCESSION RELEASES ANGELS

During a terrible time of persecution against the early church, God sent his angel to rescue the Apostle Peter from being executed by Herod. Acts chapter 12:1-11 tells this account that happens in response to the church's intersession. Let's take a look at this story and learn more about how to attract the angelic realm, beginning with Acts 12:1-5:

> Now about that time Herod the king stretched out his hand to harass some from the church. Then he killed James the brother of John with the sword. And because he saw that it pleased the Jews, he proceeded further to seize Peter also. Now it was during the Days of Unleavened Bread. So when he had arrested him, he put him in prison, and delivered him to four squads of soldiers to keep him, intending to bring him before the people after Passover. Peter was therefore kept in prison, but constant prayer was offered to God for him by the church.

This passage of scripture shows us the importance of having others pray on our behalf. There is power in the unison of prayer. I encourage people to raise up intercessors to pray on their behalf in all that they do in life, regardless of their occupation. This is especially important for those who are ministers. Ministers need to have lots of prayer covering because they are doing God's work.

If you are going to fight on the frontlines of the army of God, you must have powerful intercessors to help partner with you in prayer so that you may accomplish all that God wants you to. I know, personally, that my wife and I would not be able to do all that we do without the prayers and intercession of others. (Please pray for us as we take the Gospel of Jesus Christ to the nations of the world.)

The story continues in Acts 12:6-7:

> *And when Herod was about to bring him out, that night Peter was sleeping, bound with two chains between two soldiers; and the guards before the door were keeping the prison. Now behold, an angel of the Lord stood by him, and a light shone in the prison; and he struck Peter on the side and raised him up, saying, "Arise quickly!" And his chains fell off his hands.*

I love this part of the story. This portion of scripture demonstrates that when angels come on assignment from heaven, they *do not* waste time. When this angel suddenly shows up, he slaps Peter on the side and tells him to wake up. This angel means business! The amazing thing is that Peter's chains immediately fall off as the angel invades the prison cell—even with the guards being *right there*! When angels show up on the scene, freedom immediately happens.

Let's look at the rest of this testimony:

> *Then the angel said to him, "Gird yourself and tie on your sandals"; and so he did. And he said to him, "Put on your garment and follow me." So he went out and followed him, and did not know that what was done by the angel was*

real, but thought he was seeing a vision. When they were past the first and the second guard posts, they came to the iron gate that leads to the city, which opened to them of its own accord; and they went out and went down one street, and immediately the angel departed from him. And when Peter had come to himself, he said, "Now I know for certain that the Lord has sent His angel, and has delivered me from the hand of Herod and from all the expectation of the Jewish people." So, when he had considered this, he came to the house of Mary, the mother of John whose surname was Mark, where many were gathered together praying. (Acts 12:8-12)

As the angel leads Peter out of his cell and through the gates to his freedom, Peter doesn't even realize what's happening. The apostle thinks it's a dream or a vision. Finally he realizes that God actually sent an *angel* to rescue him. Like Peter, we don't always have to know what we are doing; we just need to trust God and be obedient to His voice when He speaks. Peter could have argued or panicked when the angel showed up; instead he did everything the angel told him to do without question, and the result was freedom from the plans of his enemies.

The cool part is that God led Peter to the very place where they were praying and interceding for his freedom, and everyone was shocked and built up in their faith as they saw that God responds to corporate intercession and prayer (see Acts 12:13-19).

Have your intercessors pray for the angels of heaven to be around you at all times and to be active in all that you do. You will see and feel the difference in your family, business, or ministry.

PRAYER AND FASTING

Praying and fasting is another way to attract heaven's help. Like I mentioned earlier, in Daniel 10 the prophet received a great breakthrough as he was fasting and crying out for his generation. He had fasted for twenty-one days and nights, and at the end of that time the angel Gabriel appeared to him.

Gabriel told Daniel that the moment the prayers left Daniel's lips, his Father in heaven had already answered them. Gabriel went on to tell Daniel that he would have come quicker had not the prince of Persia stood against him to resist his coming.

Because of this resistance, God had to send Michael, a warring angel, to take the prince of Persia out and *then* the answer to Daniel's prayer could safely reach him (see Daniel 10:11-13).

Sometimes when we need a breakthrough, we are actually in need of angelic assistance, along with fasting and intense prayer. This powerful combination can loose the angels on our behalf to bring the breakthrough we are waiting for. It's through times like this when breakthrough happens and when God will quicken the answers to our prayers.

> Sometimes when we need a breakthrough, we are actually in need of angelic assistance, along with fasting and intense prayer!

Fasting can also get us out of the flesh and more in tune with the spiritual realm so we can clearly see what we are dealing with. When we see and understand what's going on in the spirit, we will know when to bind the demonic and loose the angelic. Jesus said that whatever you bind on earth will be bound in heaven, and whatever you loose on earth will be loosed in heaven (see Matthew 16:19).

INTIMACY AND A GENEROUS HEART

Another way to attract heaven's attention and receive visitations from God and the angelic realm is to carry the heart of the Father. One thing I admire about God is that He is a lover of people and He has a generous heart. You can see this in the most foundational scripture to Christianity: John 3:16 shows us the heart of God the Father. It says,

> For God so loved the world that He gave His only begotten
> Son, that whoever believes in Him should not perish but
> have everlasting life.

We can catch the heart of God through this scripture. He loves people and He gave His all for them in sacrificing His own Son. If we as God's people can begin to live in such a way that we demonstrate true love to people, the realm of heaven will be attracted to us.

Cornelius was a man who carried the Father's heart. In Acts 10 this particular Roman centurion of the Italian Regiment received a mighty visitation from an angel; this angelic encounter precipitating the Apostle Peter coming to his house to preach. As a result, Cornelius' whole household was saved and they became the first gentile family to be born again.

Why did heaven choose Cornelius as the man to have this amazing visitation of an angel? A visitation, more importantly, that brought forth salvation not only for him, but also for his family? Let's take a look at Acts 10:1-5 and find out:

> *There was a certain man in Caesarea called Cornelius, a centurion of what was called the Italian Regiment, a devout man and one who feared God with all his household, who gave alms generously to the people, and prayed to God always. About the ninth hour of the day he saw clearly in a vision an angel of God coming in and saying to him, "Cornelius!" And when he observed him, he was afraid, and said, "What is it, lord?" So he said to him, "Your prayers and your alms have come up for a memorial before God. Now send men to Joppa, and send for Simon whose surname is Peter.*

In this scripture passage, the first thing to note is Cornelius' *intimacy* before the Lord. Acts 10:2 says that Cornelius feared the Lord, prayed to God always, and gave alms generously to people. Clearly, Cornelius was a lover of God who walked in the fear of the Lord and whose prayer life was on fire! If you want to attract the attention of the King and His Kingdom, you have to value intimacy with Him as your *greatest* treasure.

Secondly, if you want to have visitations like Cornelius, you have to make time for *prayer*. Cornelius lived a lifestyle of prayer and spent time with God. Follow this man's example, and I can assure you God will encounter you because your focus will be right.

The third thing to pay attention to in this passage is the *generosity* of Cornelius. The Scriptures say that he gave alms (or finances) to those who were in need. A generous heart grabs heaven's attention. This *does not* mean that we can *buy* the anointing, but the Father in heaven has a generous heart and when we carry that same heart, things are released to us in the spirit.

> A generous heart grabs heaven's attention.

It's interesting that in verse 4 God tells Cornelius that his prayers (or intimacy) and his alms have come before Him as a memorial in heaven. God values generosity and intimacy, and heaven takes notice when God's people are both intimate with Him *and* generous with their finances. This is why I believe every believer should be tithing to God. It shows that we value and carry God's heart, and it builds a lasting record in heaven.

If you want an increase in visitations, be diligent about praying and giving. When you give into the kingdom of God, you reap the kingdom of God. God is after our whole hearts and one of the best ways for Him to test us in our love for Him is through our financial giving. I believe that like Cornelius, if we love God and people, and live a generous lifestyle like our Father, we will attract the attention of heaven. As a result, more kingdom activity will be released in and through our lives. This kingdom activity includes visitations of the Lord through dreams, visions and angelic encounters.

THE FEAR OF THE LORD

One of the greatest ways to attract heaven's help is to walk in the fear of the Lord. This is one of the keys of Cornelius' walk with God. Acts 10:2 says that Cornelius was a devout man who feared the Lord along with his entire household. When we honor God and who He is in our lives, all of heaven is attracted to us, especially His angels.

Psalm 34:7 tells us that the fear of the Lord attracts the angels of heaven: "The angel of the LORD encamps all around those who fear Him, and delivers them."

When we honor the King of glory more then anything else in our lives, and we live lifestyles pleasing to God, loving Him more than anything, we attract visitations. Purity is the byproduct of the fear of the Lord and honoring the King. This purity draws the visitation realm.

(I will go into more depth on the fear of the Lord and how it attracts heaven's attention in chapter 11, "Angels of Awakening".)

OBEDIENCE ATTRACTS ANGELS

Intimacy with God and obedience to His voice releases or attracts the supernatural. This is a rule of thumb that I have personally experienced. If we can learn to be led of the Holy Spirit and be obedient to His voice, we will see supernatural things take place in both our lives and in the lives of those around us.

I have noticed that when I say "yes" to God and am obedient to His voice, He visits me and gives me insight and direction for my life. God will often speak to me about a certain nation before He opens up the door and sends me to it.

> Purity is the byproduct of the fear of the Lord and honoring the King.

When I am obedient to go where God directs, I often experience visitations from Him.

It's like when I shared earlier about the visitation of the angel representing Korea. In that case, the angel gave me specific insight into effectively ministering to the Korean people. It was *after* I said "yes" to the Holy Spirit about going to Korea that the visitation took place. In fact, this visitation took place shortly after I landed and got off the plane in Seoul.

There is something powerful about being in the right place at the right time. My wife and I have had all kinds of amazing supernatural encounters as we have said "yes" to God. He has nudged us, and we have responded, as He has called us to go to the nations and preach the good news of the gospel of Jesus Christ.

I have found that there is an acceleration of wisdom and visitations when we have a heart to preach the gospel. Proverbs 11:30 says, "The fruit of the righteous is a tree of life, and he who wins souls is wise." There is wisdom in hearing God's voice and being obedient to it. You will see an increase of God's power activated in your life when you use the gifts that He has given in the ways that He intended.

> Regarding the gifts of the Spirit, I tell people that they generally work better outside of the church.

The reason why God wants to give *you* visitations and wisdom is because He wants you to know Him more; the reason why He wants to empower you with gifts such as miracles, healing, and prophesy is because he wants *others* to know Him and be saved. Regarding the gifts of the Spirit, I tell people that they generally work better outside of the church. God has called us to preach the gospel to the ends of the earth and take part in the

Great Commission by sharing the message of Jesus with the world (see Matthew 28).

You can attract the angels of heaven by having a heart to share your faith with the lost. God has a love for souls, and the angelic are attracted to whatever is in God's heart. If souls are on God's heart, then we best get a heart for souls. In fact, God has so much love for the lost that He has assigned angels just to help us win souls! The writer of the book of Hebrews wrote, "Are they not all ministering spirits sent forth to minister for those who will inherit salvation?" (Hebrews 1:14)

This scripture shows us that one of the major functions of the angels of heaven is to assist us in winning souls and bringing people to know Jesus as their Lord and Savior.

Some of the most incredible angelic activity we have seen has been when we are out on the mission field. One of the things that both my wife and I love to do is to lead teams of people on trips where we do large soul-winning events (or healing campaigns) for Christ.

For more than seven years we have been leading teams to different places like Peru, Ecuador, Brazil, Africa, Indonesia and many other corners of the globe. As we have gone, we have noticed that there is always a heightened sense of angelic activity. Many people that have come on these trips with us have been activated in the supernatural in amazing ways. People that have never seen creative miracles like blind eyes opening, deaf ears hearing, or even the lame or paralyzed walking, will start to see these kinds of things happen through them when they come on these trips.

One of the most common things that take place is the release of unusual visitations from heaven. A lot of times, people testify to either seeing angels for the first time or to experiencing God in a radical way during the night—often in a dream. My wife and I find that visitations of the Lord seem to happen more as we are preaching or winning souls in the nations.

My wife Miranda always seems to have crazy encounters with God when we go to Southeast Asia and minister in places like Singapore and Indonesia. On more then a few occasions she has had angelic visitations as well as encounters with Jesus while we were in those nations preaching the gospel. This is why I believe that obedience to the Great Commission causes us to attract the attention of heaven and especially the angels of God.

When preaching in meetings or open-air crusades in places like Africa and India, I have seen the angels of heaven flying in from far and wide to be a part of our meetings. I am not quite sure if God is just sending in reinforcements (i.e. "His heavenly troops") on our behalf, *or* if these angelic beings were just curious as to what was going on in the natural realm. I have, at times, gotten a strong sense of the latter.

> I have found that doing kingdom things like preaching the gospel releases kingdom things like miracles and angelic activity.

I have found that doing kingdom things like preaching the gospel releases kingdom things like miracles and angelic activity. This is evident through the life and testimony of the great evangelist, Philip, in the New Testament of the Bible. The book of Acts shows us that Philip was a man who had a love for sharing the gospel, but he was also a man of supernatural power graced to him by God.

As you look at Philip's life, you will notice that he was radically obedient to God and did whatever God asked him to do. As a result, he had amazing heavenly visitations and was used by God to bring many to Christ. Now let's take a look and see what Philip's life and ministry looked like through the Word:

> *Now an angel of the Lord spoke to Philip, saying, "Get up and go south to the road that descends from Jerusalem to Gaza." (This is a desert road.)* (Acts 8:26 NASB)

In this portion of scripture we can see that Philip received supernatural direction from heaven; one key to his ministry was his obedience to this angelic direction. One function of the angels of God is to lead us to people whose hearts are open and ready to hear the gospel message. We already know that Philip was a man of obedience because earlier in the gospels God told him to go to Samaria and preach there. When he did, revival broke out. Directly after that happened, this encounter took place.

Like I mentioned earlier, if you do kingdom things (like preach the gospel), kingdom things happen. Visitations, miracles and supernatural direction from heaven happen when we align ourselves with heaven's mandate and do kingdom things. We still need godly confidence and boldness to step out and be obedient. We also need spiritual guidance and accountability, as well as a cloak of intercession surrounding us. I also believe that as we are faithful with little, God will give us much.

Look what happened as Philip was obedient to the angel that came to him:

> *So he arose and went. And behold, a man of Ethiopia, a eunuch of great authority under Candace the queen of the Ethiopians, who had charge of all her treasury, and had come to Jerusalem to worship, was returning. And sitting in his chariot, he was reading Isaiah the prophet. Then the Spirit said to Philip, "Go near and overtake this chariot."* (Acts 8: 27-29)

As Philip is obedient to the direction that came by the angelic visitation, he is led directly to a man of great importance who is ready to receive Jesus as Lord and Savior. To start, Philip headed in the direction that God had told him to go. The Spirit then tells Philip to overtake the Ethiopian's chariot.

The result was salvation for the Ethiopian man and supernatural transportation for Philip. After overtaking the Ethiopian's chariot, Philip ends up baptizing the man in water and is immediately (as he was baptizing this new convert) transported from one place to another. It was instantaneous, not progressive. This is completely supernatural and it happened *as* he was baptizing the Ethiopian man:

> *Now when they came up out of the water, the Spirit of the LORD caught Philip away, so that the eunuch saw him no more; and he went on his way rejoicing. But Philip was found at Azotus. And passing through, he preached in all the cities till he came to Caesarea.* (Acts 8:39-40)

This proves that intimacy with God and obedience to His voice attracts the angels of heaven and the supernatural activities of God. Just like Philip, you can attract the attention of heaven and the angelic realm by developing a heart that is open to sharing the gospel wherever you go.

A PRAYER FOR YOU:

Lord, help me to live a lifestyle of intimacy with You that attracts heaven's attention in my everyday life. Give me a fresh hunger for intimacy with the King of the kingdom and teach me to be radically obedient to Your voice, in Jesus' name. Amen.

10

ANGELS THAT RELEASE THE JUSTICE OF GOD

had a dream one night where God began to show me that through the principles of justice, He would raise up an army of champions for His glory. The Lord revealed that the angels of heaven would play a large part in bringing and releasing heaven's justice on the earth. So what was the dream?

In this powerful night encounter, I dreamt I was lying in a huge room filled with about twenty bunk beds. The room had one big window and the walls were made of cement. I knew that I was in an army barrack that housed the army of God. Soldiers were sleeping in their beds, resting for the next training day. I could see the army fatigues and boots neatly folded at the foot of each bed. I knew that this was a boot camp where God was training and equipping His army for war.

Beside every sleeping soldier's bunk bed was a night table containing peoples' personal belongings. I was the only one awake in the dream, and as I looked closely to the left of my bunk, I discovered that I too had a night table beside my bunk with several of my personal items on it. Three things on the table stood out to me, each of which belonged to me—my wedding ring, my favorite watch, and my wallet. Immediately after discovering this table beside my bed, I heard the window in the room being forced open.

I watched as a man dressed in black with a black ski mask covering his face, crawled through the window into the room. I instantly understood that this man was a thief who had broken into the room to steal from the sleeping men. The thief did not notice me watching him so I pretended to be asleep. As I acted like I was sleeping, the thief crept around, beginning to steal each sleeping soldier's personal items. He moved from night table to night table, robbing valuable items and sticking them into his sack.

As soon as the thief approached my night table, I threw my covers off, jumped out of my bed and wrestled the man to the ground. I put the thief into a headlock and he immediately passed out. I then looked around and observed a table in the room with a phone resting on it. I knew that I needed to pick up the phone and report the thief to my authorities.

When I picked up the phone the scene changed and I was no longer in the bunkroom with the other solders; I was now in a huge courtroom. There was a court case in progress. As I looked to the center of the room I saw that Jesus was present. He was beautiful and dressed in a judge's robe. I was amazed as I realized that I now stood before the Righteous Judge of all heaven and earth. I realized that I was a part of this great trial. I also saw that the thief I had just wrestled into submission was now standing in the courtroom.

Jesus looked intently at the thief and declared, "You were caught in the very act! Now sevenfold justice must be recompensed." Jesus slammed down the court gavel and I watched as angels were immediately sent to bring His proclamation to pass. The vision ended with Jesus smiling at me, as if I had won an amazing victory for God.

After this dream, God began to speak to me about the sevenfold justice of God. As He did, I realized that God cares immensely about everything that goes on in our lives. He especially cares when we have been ripped off and stolen from by the enemy. The Lord told me that He would raise up an army for Himself through the principles of justice. He would use the very attacks of the devil as tools to empower His people. God's soldiers would overcome the enemy's attacks and the kingdom of darkness and that His army would shine forth Christ's light.

Proverbs 6:30-31 says that when the thief is caught stealing from God's people, he must repay sevenfold what has been taken. I realize that a lot of people in the body of Christ have been completely ripped off by the enemy. In my dream, the thief had stolen from all of those who were *asleep* in the bunkroom; they were innocent victims and most of them had no clue what had happened.

I had caught the thief in my dream and then called upon my authority, Jesus Christ, to help me. God wants his people to call on Him for help in times of warfare. God doesn't want you to get beaten up. When I took authority over the devil and called upon Jesus in my dream, God released justice on my behalf. As soon as that happened, the angels of heaven were sent to change my situation.

Like I said earlier in this book, one of the main functions of angelic beings is to perform God's word on the earth. Psalm 103:20 says, "Bless the Lord, you His angels, who excel in strength, who do His word, heeding the voice of His word!"

God used this experience to show me what happens when we know *who* we are and *whose* we are in Christ. When we ask God for justice against our enemy and walk in our God-given authority as believers, not giving up in times of trials and warfare, the angels of heaven are sent on our behalf to bring a breakthrough of sevenfold justice on our behalf. If you are going through tough times and warfare, cry out to the righteous judge of heaven and earth and ask Him for justice. Ask God to release the host of heaven to recompense the things that have been stolen from you.

Recently I put these principles into practice. I remember being on a trip to Argentina not long ago, and when I was there, I left my iPad at a coffee shop right before we went to a meeting. When I was in the middle of the meeting it dawned on me that I had forgotten my iPad. As soon as the meeting was over we went and asked the shop owners if they had found an iPad and they told us they had not.

My translator told the owner of the shop that I was a minister and that we needed to get the iPad back, but the man swore that he did not have the iPad. We finally left the café with me feeling disheartened, ripped off by the devil, and like the shop owner was lying about the iPad. When I returned to my hotel that night, I remember looking all over my room, hoping that the iPad would turn up.

I tore open my suitcase and thoroughly searched it, but found my iPad nowhere; I was grieved. I know it's just a possession but this iPad carried all of my notes for every one of my messages that I spoke and released around the world. Needless to say, this tool was priceless to me.

We ended up having to pack everything up and travel to another city. I felt completely ripped off but at the same time, I felt a bit stupid for being so careless with my iPad in a developing country. While we were driving to the next city, I prayed to God and asked Him for justice regarding what had been stolen from me.

I prayed earnestly, decreeing scriptures over the situation and asking God to move. We eventually stopped and checked into a hotel for the night. When my roommate and I got to our new hotel room, I told him that I had faith God was about to do a miracle for me, so I said, "Let's pray." I looked at my suitcase and made a decree over it, saying, "In the name of Jesus, I command my iPad to come back to me!"

I opened my bag and right before both my roommate and me, the iPad appeared! We were so excited, we screamed! This was a perfect example of the justice of God manifesting immediately, right in front of our eyes. I had spent 20 minutes tearing through my bag and hotel room in search of my iPad before we had left the old hotel, only to leave discouraged and disheartened.

With this lack of success in my thorough search, there was no possible way *in the natural* that this little electronic device could have been in the bag. However, when the justice of God manifested, I knew that God had sent an angel to get the iPad back from whoever had stolen it from me. I understood that when we made the decree, the angel brought it back to me and God had answered my prayer for justice.

Some of you have had things lost or stolen from you; you need to use your authority and call these things back in the name of Jesus. When you do this, God will send His angels on assignment and manifest missing things back to you. The Lord will give you justice and return to you that which was stolen, even if it was stolen by the devil. I can only imagine the possible situation of the person who stole my iPad—he could have been playing games on it when suddenly an angel appeared right before his eyes, snatched back the iPad and then disappeared again out of the thief's sight. It's possible!

I realize that some of you have lost things that make my iPad episode look almost trivial. Some of you have lost spouses to infidelity, sickness or death. Others of you have lost children through a prodigal journey, or perhaps even through death. And for others, perhaps you feel that your destiny has been ripped off due to unemployment, betrayal, disability, or addiction.

While the scars of these types of losses go deep, we serve a Lord who is in the business of redemption. Though you might not ever have these physical things redeemed in this life, the Lord nonetheless wants to restore your destiny now—by you allowing Him to enter your heart and bring healing to your grieving and broken places.

God is an amazing God and it wouldn't be surprising if He would have used my situation to not only release justice to me, but also to teach the thief a powerful lesson in not stealing from men of God. This would have been an amazing witness to the reality of God. Let's start calling back lost items and decreeing justice over our situations—whether the loss was physical, emotional, or spiritual.

The angels of God are sent to bring these things back to God's children! I heard another story similar to mine from one of my spiritual fathers, Bobby Conner, about how an angel brought him his wives clothes that he had lost on a plane. Check out this testimony out of his book called *Angels*.

> Let's start calling back lost items and decreeing justice over our situations—whether the loss was physical, emotional, or spiritual.

BOBBY CONNER ANGEL TESTIMONY

Well-respected prophet Bobby Conner relayed this story to me one day:

> A while ago, my wife, Carolyn, and I were on a ministry trip, and we had extremely tight flight schedules. After landing in an airport, we rushed to catch our next plane at a distant terminal. In the rush, I forgot to get Carolyn's clothes, which I had hung up on the previous plane. Only after boarding our next flight, just moments from departure, did I realize my mistake.
>
> I needed to retrieve her clothing, so I got off the plane, thinking that if I missed that flight I would just catch the later flight. However, as I started down the jet

bridge to exit the plane, suddenly the most pleasing lady appeared in the jet way with my wife's clothing bags.

"Here Pastor Conner are Carolyn's clothes," she said. I was shocked that she knew our names, and after I started back into the plane, I turned around again to thank her and ask how she knew me. When I did, I discovered that I was totally alone on the jet bridge. She had vanished in a moment.

When I got back on the plane, Carolyn said with a puzzled expression, "How did you get back so quickly?" I explained what had happened, which I am convinced was an encounter with an angel who helped us retrieve Carolyn's clothing, allowing us to still make our flight.

Thank God for the help of heaven. If you have lost something of importance to you or a family member, or if the devil has stolen something from you, then cry out to God to release his angels on assignment in order to release to you the sevenfold justice of God.

A PRAYER FOR YOU

Lord, I ask You for sevenfold justice for everything the devil has stolen from me and from my family. I ask you to loose the angels of heaven on my behalf and bring breakthrough into every area of my life. I call back those things that have been stolen or lost in Jesus' mighty name. Amen.

11

ANGELS OF AWAKENING

Four years ago, a prophet named Bob Jones gave me a prophetic word that I was to wait on the Lord on Yom Kippur and that God the Father would visit me on that date. The prophecy said God would release revelation concerning what He was about to do in His church over that next year. I took that word to heart and since then, the Lord has consistently visited me on Yom Kippur. Over the last several years, I have had either angelic visitations, or even encounters with Jesus Christ.

This year was no different. While I was praying and waiting on the Lord on the evening of September 25th, which was Yom Kippur, I fell into a trance and was caught up into an encounter with God. I found myself standing before this massive door in heaven that was about five times bigger then any earthly door I had ever seen. I also noticed in big bold letters written over the top of the door the word BREAKTHROUGH.

Jesus appeared dressed in all white, with a blue sash about his chest. He grabbed me by the hand and walked me up to this massive door. Then, with a huge smile on His face, He reached into a pocket in His garment, pulled out a set of keys, handed them to me and told me to unlock the massive door. As I grabbed the keys, I noticed that one key in particular bore a scripture written along the shaft of the key. That scripture was Habakkuk 2:14: "For the earth will be filled with the knowledge of the glory of the LORD, as the waters cover the sea."

I knew I was to insert the key of Habakkuk 2:14 to open the door.

As I turned the key, I heard the sound of the deadbolt of this massive door slide back, echoing throughout all the heavenly realms. Then without thinking about it, I started pulling on this massive door, trying to open it. But I could not. I pulled and pulled with all of my strength and the door only cracked open about a half inch. The brilliant light of God's glory seeped through the crack. I pulled all the more on the door but could not get it to open any further.

Then all of a sudden, Jesus reached out and touched my shoulder saying, "Take three steps back and watch what I do."

So in obedience I took three steps back. I heard a sound like a freight train coming from inside the door. Then within a matter of seconds, a violent wind hit the back of the door and blew it wide open. The wind hit with such velocity that it almost knocked the door off its hinges.

Out of the wind materialized an angel that I somehow knew was an "Angel of Awakening." The large angel stared at me. I looked into his eyes and I could see hundreds of thousands of angels that looked just like him, being released into the earth. Then, I looked over at Jesus and saw a huge smile of delight on His face.

Since the time of the visitation, the Lord has been speaking to me about the Church and the Angel of Awakening releasing the keys of revelation knowledge—keys that will open the doors to an increase in the glory of God.

A WORD FOR THE CHURCH TODAY

I believe we are in a season of open doors. God is going to release keys of revelation regarding the things on His heart, as well as knowledge concerning the glory of God.

The key to opening this massive door in the spirit is found in Habakkuk 2:14. That scripture says that the *knowledge* of the glory of God will cover the whole earth as the waters cover the sea. The scripture does not say that the *glory of the Lord* is going to cover the earth. We need to understand what this scripture is saying.

Revelation knowledge is different from head knowledge. What we know in our mind about God and His kingdom, and what we know and believe about Him in our hearts are often two different things. God is about to take what we know in our heads and activate it in our hearts and lives to see

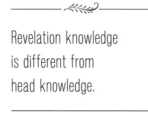

Revelation knowledge is different from head knowledge.

the door of breakthrough open up for our destinies and callings!

God is about to do for His people what we cannot do for ourselves. That is why Jesus told me to step back and watch what He does. As I took a step back from trying to open the door of break-through in my own strength, He broke it open by sending heaven's help as an angel of awakening broke the door down.

I believe that we are in a season of receiving heaven's help at this time in the body of Christ. We cannot operate without the help of angels releasing the knowledge of the glory of God and facilitating breakthroughs in individual lives and in nations.

Hebrews 1:14 tells us that God's angels are ministering spirits sent to assist those who are to inherit salvation. In my encounter, I knew that the angel standing next to Jesus was an angel of awakening. As I looked into the angel's eyes I could see hundreds of thousands of other angels that looked just like the one standing in front of me. God is releasing "angels of awakening" to His church. Who will these angels visit? You? Maybe. Are you ready to wake up?

A BALANCE BETWEEN THE LOVE OF GOD AND THE FEAR OF THE LORD

You are probably wondering if you even want this angel to show up in your life. What will this Angel of Awakening do in your life, or in the lives of those around you? Get ready for total transformation . . .

Psalm 34:7 states that the angel of the Lord encamps around those who fear Him, and delivers them. I felt the Holy Spirit tell me that the Father is now commissioning angels of awakening to His people—and the awakening involves understanding how to walk in the love of God and the fear of the Lord.

These angels will be assigned and released to those who walk in the love and fear of God, or are willing to do so. Partnering with these angels will release individuals into their destinies and bring an awakening through them, to the world. Get ready for a healthy balance between the fear of the Lord and the love of God, as revelation knowledge begins to reveal the truth about these two aspects of God.

The message of extreme grace being preached in certain churches fails to understand the concept of the fear of the Lord. Truly understanding these two aspects of God's nature will result in genuine passion and intimacy with God. The awe of God's glory and presence releases both a sense of God's love and a holy fear. While it is God's love that brings us to repentance, fear of the Lord often empowers the grace of God in the life of a believer.

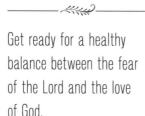

Get ready for a healthy balance between the fear of the Lord and the love of God.

If we can begin to understand the way love and fear empowers grace, we will be able to attract heaven's attention and help. Lets look at what the grace of God is and what it is not. People tend to think that the grace of God has to do with covering their sins. People with this understanding say stuff like, "Just have grace on me" or, "I'm just a sinner saved by grace."

Grace has nothing to do with forgiving your sins, and your identity is not to be built around being labeled a "sinner." We are called sons and daughters of God. The reality is that the blood of Jesus provides the forgiveness of our sins—not grace. Grace is given not to forgive your sins but rather to empower you to stay out of sin.

So many Christians are just looking for an excuse to sin and not walk in the fear of the Lord. They have no concept of the fear of the

Lord. The fear of the Lord is what gets heaven's attention. It is also that which will empower God's grace in a believer's life.

A true definition of the fear of the Lord is not legalism. It is not the school of thought that says, *don't do this* and *don't do that* or God is going to strike you or punish you in some way. The fear of the Lord is simply to fall in love with Jesus with all of your heart and out of that love, you don't want to behave in self-defeating ways or harm your relationship with Jesus.

Fear enables you to determine that the way you live your life will be according to what pleases Him. Your heart says, *I am so in love with Jesus that I don't want to hurt his heart.* That is our motivation for not doing the things that we should not.

When we carry this heart full of the love of God it will empower grace in our lives to overcome every temptation that the devil would toss our way to trip us up. It's this kind of walk that attracts the attention of heaven—not a lifestyle of judgment and legalism. When you are in love with Jesus you will naturally live in a place of the fear of the Lord where you naturally carry a heart that is set on Him and pleases Him.

WAKING UP TO GREATER GLORY

When you are awakened from slumber and death, into the light and love of God's resurrection power, you will never be the same. You will want more of God's glory just like I did in my dream. I only glimpsed the light of God's glory, but that small glimpse made me want to open that door quickly. Then, in a matter of seconds, ***boom***!

Breakthrough happened as heaven's help broke down that seemingly impossible door. It was as if the light of Christ broke through: "Awake, you who sleep, arise from the dead, and Christ will give you light" (see Ephesians 5:14).

God is sending heaven's angels to those who have felt like they have seen very little light and satisfaction in their walk with God. He is about to breathe life into those believers who feel they are in a place of hope deferred, which has made their hearts sick (see Proverbs 13:12). He is about to crush every obstacle or mountain that seems to be standing against destinies. Lost or stolen promises of God will not only be restored, but also fulfilled!

Get ready for things that have felt dead or dormant to come back to life as the light of His glory shines in this season. Things like your giftings, anointing, calling and even your faith will be restored as God the father releases His angels of awakening!

Zechariah 4 is a "now" promise for us in this season of open doors. God is going to release to the Church the power of His Spirit to speak to the mountains of hopelessness, sickness, and disease as well as the strongholds of the enemy. Watch them bow to the name of Jesus.

As I was praying about the purposes of these angels of awakening, the Lord led me to the book of Zechariah. In Zechariah 4:1-5, God the Father sent an angel that awakened Zechariah out of slumber as a man is awakened out of His sleep. As I read, I realized that God was giving me a blueprint of what He was about to do in the body of Christ in this hour. Let's take a look at this portion of scripture and break it down.

Now the angel who talked with me came back and wakened me, as a man who is wakened out of his sleep. And he said to me, "What do you see?" So I said, "I am looking, and there is a lampstand of solid gold with a bowl on top of it, and on the stand seven lamps with seven pipes to the seven lamps. Two olive trees are by it, one at the right of the bowl and the other at its left." So I answered and spoke to the angel who talked with me, saying, "What are these, my lord?" Then the angel who talked with me answered and said to me, "Do you not know what these are?" And I said, "No, my lord."

This portion of scripture reveals God's motivation to send angels of awakening to his people in Zechariah's season—but also to our generation. I also believe it brings some definition to what *awakening* is going to do in the body of Christ.

Zechariah's heavenly encounter happened during a time when rebellion and a massive falling away from God plagued the church. We know this because in Zechariah 3, the great high priest Joshua who represented the nation of Israel came before God and Satan wearing filthy garments—representing sin.

The angel of the Lord, who is a prophetic picture of Jesus, removed the sin from him (see Zechariah 3). This evolved into Zechariah experiencing this visitation, and obtaining heaven's answer to how God was bringing breakthrough to his entire generation—to bring them out of rebellion and back into the promises of God.

Zechariah received a revelation of three things: The first was an awareness of the Holy Spirit when he saw the lampstand of God in the throne room. The second was the Angel who spoke the answer to Israel's problem, when he said, "Not by might nor by power, but by my Spirit" (see Zechariah 4:6). Finally, the angel proclaimed that the mountain would be leveled into a plain.

This angel of awakening declared that the obstacles standing in front of Zechariah have been dealt with and with that declaration, breakthrough happened. Zechariah understood that the natural ruins of the temple of God would be restored when the Messiah (or capstone) is released. Nobody else in Zechariah's generation had hoped for the restoration of the house of God, but the Lord showed Zechariah the power of the resurrection of Christ and the power of the Holy Spirit being released into the lives of His people in the aftermath. Zechariah saw how God was about to turn around the dark state of the church.

Even now, God is releasing angels of awakening to wake up His church and the world to the power of the Holy Spirit.

When believers know the Holy Spirit, they will have the ability to see things from God's perspective. They will call forth that which is not, as if it were. These angels of awakening will bring revelation to people to see things the way God sees situations. What looks hopeless in the natural will fade as faith rises when your spiritual eyes open to the activity of angels in your midst.

> When believers know the Holy Spirit, they will have the ability to see things from God's perspective.

I remember one time while speaking in Canada, a pastor asked me to pray for a man who had complete kidney failure. Many people had already prayed for this man. When I put my hands on his shoulders, I didn't know what to pray, nor did I have much faith at that time for a miracle. But my spiritual eyes opened and I saw an angel of awakening standing behind him laying hands on the man's kidneys.

I felt God tell me to put my hands where I saw the angel put his, and the power of God went right through the man's body. Instantly, the man reported that he felt better and went to the restroom for the first time in a year without pain. Later, he went to the doctors and they declared him to be a walking miracle—it looked to them as if he had brand new kidneys. This angelic visitation released a "whole life" healing: faith awakened in his life from that point on. He went from struggling to become the town evangelist, his testimony leading many to salvation.

This is what happens when an angel of awakening shows up—power is released and people are transformed. They step into their spiritual identity as sons and daughters of God, empowered to change the world.

Even if we don't know what to do, the Holy Spirit's direction will manifest at the moment we need it. And when it does, we will be able to speak to the mountains of sickness, financial despair, spiritual and relational problems, and all the things that stand in front of us or in peoples' lives around us.

The final thing the angels of awakening will do is bring people into a greater revelation of Jesus as the capstone—the One who brings shouts of grace; grace to a generation. What Zechariah was seeing was what would take place in the days of Jesus. He was seeing Jesus' defeat—once and for all—the mountain of sin and death in a day. Zechariah then saw Jesus giving us access to the same spirit that raised Him from the dead (see Acts 2).

God is about to send heaven's help to deal with the things that seem like mountains in your life. Whatever those things are, get ready for breakthrough. Ultimately, the angels of heaven are going to lift high the revelation of Jesus as Lord and Savior to this generation. Then we will see a mighty harvest of souls that will pour into the kingdom of God! As a result, Jesus will receive the fullness of the rewards of His suffering.

WAR RESULTS IN ENTIRE NATIONS COMING TO CHRIST

The book of Matthew tells us that the end times will separate the "sheep nations" and the "goat nations" (see Matthew 25:31-36). War is a part of this separation.

When the angels of heaven are released to do war in the spirit realm, heaven gets released onto earth. God is about to release angels of war alongside the angels of awakening. We can look forward to amazing days of warfare and glory. If you walk in the love of God, you will not fear the events that happen around you. The eyes of your spirit will open to see the angelic activity on earth, and you will be able to partner with them, doing what you see your Father in heaven releasing through you.

God is binding the powers and principalities that occupy entire nations who veil peoples' hearts from knowing Christ and God's love. Then the angels of awakening will come in to awaken love and many will come into the knowledge of Jesus Christ. You can see this in action already in the world.

I believe Japan was an example of what I am talking about. I was in Australia ministering the weekend that the 2011 tsunami hit Japan. There was much discussion about why this disaster happened. I remember some saying that God was judging people's sins, and others that said it was just a natural disaster and it had nothing to do with God.

I asked the Lord what happened with Japan in prayer one day and instantly, the Lord took me into an open vision. He showed me two warring angels fighting with the strongman over Japan. I watched as these two powerful angels wrestled against this principality in the heavenly realm.

As I watched this fierce battle in the spirit, the two angels of war overcame this principality, bound it, and then threw it out of the second heaven. The strongman over Japan hit the waters of the ocean causing a massive earthquake to happen resulting in the tsunami that hit Japan.

The power of the strong man was shattered when he fell out of the second heaven. Unfortunately, the nation of Japan was shattered as well. Then I watched as the Lord dispatched awakening angels over the nation of Japan to bring many to salvation.

After the vision, the Lord said, "Son, the result of the earthquake and tsunami in Japan was a direct result of the prayers of the saints in Korea. As the nation of Korea had been praying for years for Japan to have revival, I answered their prayers and the demonic stronghold over the nation of Japan broke that day."

I asked the Lord where the Bible confirmed this revelation. And the Lord led me to Haggai 2:6-7. That scripture reads,

> *For thus says the LORD of hosts: 'Once more (it is a little while) I will shake heaven and earth, the sea and dry land; and I will shake all nations, and they shall come to the Desire of All Nations, and I will fill this temple with glory,' says the LORD of hosts.*

I was amazed as God spoke this to me. It was exactly what happened to the nation of Japan. God shook the heavens, the earth, the sea, and the dry lands, and the result was an awakening to the desire of all nations, Jesus.

GOD'S JUDGMENTS DO NOT LOOK LIKE WHAT SO MANY IMAGINE

The power released was not a judgment on people. God was judging the spirits and the evil power that prevented people from knowing Him.

One of the other things the Lord told me was that when there is a collision in the realm of the spirit between God and the powers of darkness, it's not God who hits the ground, but the devil. The result is freedom over cities, peoples, and nations.

I believe we are currently seeing the result of this prophetic vision coming to pass. I believe God has dispatched angels of awakening over Japan since the disaster happened. More missionaries and Christians have gone to Japan than ever before in history.

In fact, there have been more churches planted and more salvations since the disaster than ever in the history of Japan. In addition, most of the first people to respond in the aftermath of the tsunami were Christian organizations who were able to help rescue and save many victims.

JAPAN HAS OPENED UP TO JESUS LIKE NEVER BEFORE

When God brings down strongholds over cities or nations, a natural repercussion happens as a result of what has taken place in the spirit. Look at what happened when Christ died on the cross and broke the powers of sin and death, once and for all, over humanity.

The same type of thing happened in His day as did with Japan. The Bible says that when Jesus proclaimed that it was finished and breathed his last breath, the earth shook violently and many of the saints of old who had passed away came up out of their graves, awoke from the slumber of death, and began to walk. I believe this was a sign that the power of death was defeated that day.

The Bible also tells us that as the powers of hell were broken that day, the centurions and guards felt the earth quake and were filled with great fear, confessing with their mouths that Jesus truly was the Son of God (see Matthew 27:50-54).

The other thing I love about this revelation is that it exposes the love of God in His judgments. So many people make our heavenly Father out to be this mean, sin-conscious God who hates sinners.

The reality is that He loves people; His judgments are not against sinners but against Satan and the powers and principalities in heavenly places that imprison people.

I believe that as God sends his angels to rip down strongholds and to assist his followers to bring awakening into the earth, we are going to see the greatest revival we have ever seen. We are going to see entire nations changed in a day like we saw with Japan. It will be up to the Christians to decide if they are going to be the first ones on the scene, full of faith and ready to help those in times of need. We are called to disciple nations.

For those who see things from Papa God's perspective, some of the greatest days of revival lay ahead—days when God lifts up the name of His Son Jesus in the earth. God wants to partner with you to bring awakening to your school, workplace and wherever your life may take you.

Are you ready for angels of awakening to be released and assigned to your life to facilitate breakthrough and awakening?

Are you ready to see God rip down strongholds, as heaven's help is dispatched over your life?

Are you ready to speak to the mountains of impossibilities that stand at your door and watch the power of the Holy Spirit cause the mountains to become planes in your sight?

What are the mountains or obstacles that are standing in your way or in the way of revival happening in your city, state or nation?

It's time to get serious about your love for Jesus and ask Him for heaven's help and breakthrough in your life.

ENDNOTES

1. Billy Graham, *Angels: Ringing Assurance That We Are Not Alone, p. 137 (Nashville: Thomas Nelson Publishers, 1996).*

2. See http://www.epm.org/resources/2010/Mar/17/have-you-ever-been-aware-presence-demons-or-angels/

3. See http://mariposarevivalcenter.org/pdfs/Word_-_portland_vision.pdf

4. Roberts Liardon, *God's Generals: Maria Woodworth-Etter (New Kensington: Whitaker House, 2000).*

JERAME NELSON
*is the founder of Living at His Feet
Ministries. He is an author, as
well as a well-known international
conference speaker and a crusade
revivalist to the nations. It's Jerame's
passion to equip the body of Christ
in the areas of hearing God's voice,
as well as walking in the supernatural power of God in everyday life.
Jerame and his wife, Miranda, live
in Pasadena, California, and work
together in the ministry to change
the lives of thousands through the
Gospel of Jesus Christ.*